THOSE WHO FOUGHT

THOSE WHO FOUGHT

AN ANTHOLOGY OF
MEDIEVAL SOURCES

EDITED BY
PETER SPEED

ITALICA PRESS
NEW YORK
1996

ITALICA PRESS, INC.

595 MAIN STREET

NEW YORK, NEW YORK 10044

LIBRARY OF CONGRESS CATALOGING-IN-PUBLICATION DATA

Those who fought / edited by Peter Speed.
      p. cm. -- (An Anthology of Medieval sources)
      Includes bibliographical references and index.
      ISBN 0-934977-39-9
      1. Feudalism--Europe--History. 2. Knights and knighthood--Europe--History. 3. Aristocracy (Social class)--Europe--History. 4. Elite (Social sciences)--Europe--History. 5. Nobility--Europe--History. 6. Social history--Medieval, 500-1500. I. Speed, Peter. II. Series: Speed, Peter. Anthology of Medieval sources.
D131.T48 1996
940.1--dc20
                                                    96-4607
                                                    CIP
                                                      AC

Printed in the United States of America

5 4 3 2 1

Cover Art: The Norman cavalry attacks the Anglo-Saxon infantry. Detail from the Bayeux Tapestry (episode 51). Musée de la Tapisserie, Bayeaux, France. Giraudon/Art Resource, NY.

Unless otherwise noted, all other artwork used by permission of source cited in List of Illustrations on p. VI.

CONTENTS

ILLUSTRATIONS

ILLUSTRATIONS

ILLUSTRATIONS

PREFACE

THIS ANTHOLOGY will consist of three volumes, *Those Who Fought,*
Those Who Worked and *Those Who Prayed,* corresponding to the
social groups into which medieval people divided themselves.
It gives me great pleasure to offer these books to the people of
the United States. Not only are many of you my friends, but a
great many more, though I am afraid I cannot identify you, must
be my distant relations. I am, of course, not unique in this. Numerous groups of people on both sides of the Atlantic have ancestors in common, so it follows that the history of medieval Europe
is your history as well as our own.

I would hate to be misunderstood here. I am fully aware that
your civilization has evolved from several, and that the European
was only one of them. Nor would I, a mere historian, try to evalu-
ate them and say which has made the most valuable contribution.
My contention is simply that as Europe has made a considerable
impact on America, it is worth your while to study its history.

The volume of source material we have inherited from the
Middle Ages is so overwhelming that an anthology like this can
contain only a tiny fraction of it. I have had to select heavily, and
these have been my criteria.

In the first place, I believe history is for interest and pleasure, so
I have chosen sources which meet these needs and will, therefore,
appeal to the general reader. At the same time, this is no collection
of trivia, so the serious student will find plenty to digest. Indeed,
most of the sources can be analyzed at whatever depth the reader
chooses.

Secondly, I think historians should avoid polemics. The world is
full of good causes, and I believe in many of them, including, for
example, racial and sexual equality, but I support them through
means other than my work as a historian. Here, my prime duty is

to reflect medieval Europe and it historical sources as accurately as I can. Now, apart from the Moors of Spain, Europe contained very few black people. I have, of course, included some Moorish sources, more especially in *Those Who Worked*, but it would have been wrong of me to let them bulk too large. With women, the problem is different. As today, they formed more than half the population, because more of them were born and they lived longer lives. However, the sources were, on the whole, written by men, for men, and about men. These are the facts of history and I cannot change them. All I can do is to allow women as large a place as the sources will allow. "Same sex" relations are an especially difficult problem, because medieval people rarely mentioned them, and most often only to condemn. I have, nonetheless, touched on them in *Those Who Prayed*.

Thirdly, I have tried to give a general overview of medieval Europe, and to illustrate my method, I would like consider the problem of introducing a stranger to the United States. A hurried tour of many places, staying nowhere long, would not be especially informative. The time would be better spent gaining acquaintance with a selection of people and groups. This would give the visitor a series of vivid experiences, from which a general picture would emerge. The problem is to make the selection representative, and when it comes to choosing sources, no two historians will agree. If, therefore, any of my critics find that their favorite documents are not here, or that their favorite authors are not quoted, then I can only express regret at their disappointment. I would, however, point out that nothing is easier than compiling a weighty list of topics which a historian should include in his book. He has the far harder problem of deciding which ones to omit. In general, I have favored those which are well known, but I have also chosen a few which are more obscure, especially where the alternatives are readily available.

Perhaps I should say a few words about my interpretation of feudalism. It is unashamedly traditional, in spite of a massive onslaught mounted recently by Susan Reynolds (*Fiefs and Vassals*, 1994). Ms. Reynolds has done a marvellous job of demolition, but

PREFACE

she has built nothing new. It may suit her to stand confused among the ruins, with nowhere to lay her head, but I am unwilling to inflict a like fate on my readers. I explore this question more fully in Chapter Two of *Those Who Fought*.

ACKNOWLEDGMENTS

The author and publishers are grateful to the following for permission to reproduce copyright material. Numbers refer to readings: Cambridge University Press, *Medieval Garner* by G.G. Coulton, 1910: 39, 77, 81, 92, 99, 109, 112, 121, 122, 125, 127, 131, 132; University of Chicago Press, *The Three Orders,* by Georges Duby, translated by Arthur Goldhammer, 1980: 1-3; Columbia University Press, *Chaucer's England* by Edith Rickert, 1948: 78, 79, 154; Garland Publishing, *Catholic Peacemakers,* Vol. 1: *From the Bible to the Era of the Crusades,* by Ronald G. Musto, 1993: 85-88, 142, 143, 155-162; *The Writings of Medieval Women* by Marcelle Thiébaux, 1994: 103, 110; Italica Press, *Barbarossa in Italy,* edited and translated by Thomas Carson, 1994: 26, 129, 130, 144; Humanities Press, *History of Feudalism* by David Herlihy, 1970: 7-9, 13, 36-38; Penguin Classics, *Chronicles of the Crusades,* M.R.B. Shaw trans., 1963: 35; Suffolk Institute of Archaeology and History, *The Household Book of Dame Alice de Bryene,* edited by V.B. Redstone, 114-120; Messers Weidenfeld and Nicolson, *The Golden Age of Burgundy,* by Joseph Calmette, 1962: 123; *Plantaganet Chronicles,* Elizabeth Hallam ed., 1986: 10, 12, 89, 101, 102, 107, 164.

I have tried to locate all holders of copyright, but should I have missed any, I apologise to them. If they will contact me through the publishers, I will do my best to make amends.

CHAPTER 1
THE THREE ORDERS

IN HIS ADMIRABLE BOOK, *The Three Orders*, the French historian Georges Duby states that "thirty or forty successive generations have imagined social perfection in the form of trifunctionality." During the Middle Ages, and beyond, "trifunctionality often meant the division of society into three orders, those who prayed, those who fought and those who worked."

This notion is stated again and again in different centuries and in different countries. Its first recorded appearance is a note written in the margin of a translation of Boethius's *On the Consolation of Philosophy*, said to be the work of Alfred the Great, king of Wessex from 871-899. The translator says the king cannot govern without tools, so he must have "men of prayer, warriors and workmen."

A hundred years later another West Saxon, Aelfric, master of the novices at Cerne Abbey in Dorset, wrote:

> 1. In this world there are three kinds of men, laboratores, oratores, bellatores. The laboratores are those who by their labor provide us with the means to live, the oratores, those who plead for us with God, the bellatores, those who protect our cities and defend our land against invading armies. The peasant must work to feed us, the soldier must do battle with our enemies, and the servant of God must pray for us and do spiritual battle with the invisible enemies. [*Lives of the Saints*, quoted in Duby, op. cit., p. 103.]

Early in the eleventh century, Adalbero, bishop of Laon in northern France, stated:

> 2. Triple then is the house of God, which is thought to be one; on earth some pray, others fight, still others work; which

1

three are joined together and may not be torn asunder; so that the function of each rests on the works of the others, each in turn assisting all. [Ibid., p. 5]

Adalbero's colleague, Gerard, bishop of Cambrai, also remarked, "From the beginning, mankind has been divided into three parts, men of prayer, farmers and men of war."

A century after Adalbero and Gerard, Gilbert, bishop of Limerick, Ireland, wrote:

3. Those within the parish church are divided into three. Of these, the ones at the apex must be regarded as oratores, and because some of them are married, we shall call them men and women. Those to the left side of the pyramid are the aratores [ploughmen], both men and women. On the right are the bellatores, men and women. I do not say that the function of women is to pray, toil and fight, but they are married to those who pray, toil and fight, and they serve them. And since the beginning the Church has recognized these three legitimate orders of the faithful, so that within it one part, the clergy, might concern itself with prayer, protecting the others against attacks of the Deceiver; another, sweating in heavy labor, may rescue the others from want of nourishment; the third, devoted to knighthood, defends the others against physical enemies. [Ibid., pp. 287-88]

We should note in passing that Gilbert's account is unusual in that he reserves a place, of a kind, for women. He also mentions the wives of clergy. During the early Middle Ages parish priests did marry, even though the church authorities frowned on the practice and passed several measures against it. For example, the Second Lateran Council, held in 1139 during the papacy of Innocent II forbade the marriage of priests. However, celibacy only became general among the lower clergy towards the end of the twelfth century and there were married priests in Iberia and Scandinavia long after that.

There are various reasons for the persistence of the notion of the three orders. The first is the appeal of the number three. It

occurs in religion, mythology and superstition. A generalized state-
ment will have more credibility, if it is backed by three specific
examples. Three suggests stability, for a three legged stool is firm,
even if it stands on uneven ground. Next, trifunctionality was a useful weapon in the hands of those
who wished to impose order and discipline. All the authors who
have been quoted felt this need. Anglo-Saxon Wessex was under
constant attack from Danish Vikings. In the time of Adalbero and
Gerard, the millennium of the Passion, the year 1031, was approaching, and this, many believed, would see the end of the world. There
was social tumult, with the collapse of royal authority and petty
lordlings who spread disorder. Gilbert of Limerick's Ireland was in
chaos, as has too often been the lot of that unhappy country.

The ideal of social discipline was embedded in the notion of
trifunctionality. Adalbero and Gerard saw the three orders as cre-
ations of the divine will. In Heaven, even angels who were without sin had to obey archangels. How much more important was
it, then, that mortals should give unquestioning obedience to their
superiors. The members of the third order, the common people,
were undoubtedly the lowest. Their duty was to minister to the
needs of the great, consoling themselves with the thought that
they were earning salvation by the pain of their labor.

While the status of the common people was clear, there was a
shift in opinion on whether the clergy or the warriors should hold
the highest place. Adalbero had no doubts. He saw the king as part
priest, by virtue of his anointing when he was crowned. He was,
though, an imperfect priest, for he was distracted by affairs of state
while, from time to time, he was obliged to use the sword. Bishops, on the other hand, devoted most of their time to things spiritual and were, moreover, in direct contact with God. Indeed, it
was not unknown for them to flaunt letters which they had received, by some mysterious postal service, direct from Heaven.
Clearly, it was the bishops' task to guide the king and it was his
duty to obey them.

Later, the concept of the three orders was desacralized. Between
1173 and 1175 Benedict of Sainte-Maure wrote a *History of the Dukes*

of Normandy. It was commissioned by Henry Plantagenet who, though King Henry II of England, was more important as a French prince, holding as he did the titles of Duke of Normandy, Count of Anjou and several others, as well as being the ruler of southwest France by virtue of his marriage to Eleanor of Aquitaine. Henry wished to assert himself against his feudal overlord the king of France, and Benedict obliged him. He shows the prince as standing above the three orders while they, no longer corresponding to the company of angels, are three pillars of state, supporting his rule. But the Plantagenet empire in France crumbled. John, king of England from 1199 to 1216, lost Normandy, Anjou, Maine and Touraine. Then, in 1214, Philip Augustus of France beat John's ally, the Emperor Otto IV of Germany, at the Battle of Bouvines. William le Breton, who was at the battle, composed his epic poem, the *Philippiad*, intending it to rival Virgil's *Aeneid*. Here, the three orders support no ordinary prince, like the duke of Normandy, but an anointed king. There were the knights, his close companions in arms, the people, who formed the rank and file of the army, and the priests, who blessed the enterprise, offered prayers and chanted psalms. Either the men of prayer or the men of war, then, could be pre-eminent, but whichever it might be, there was an ordered hierarchy with a chain of command running from top to bottom.

A third reason for the persistence of the concept of the three orders was that it had some foundation in social reality. Obviously, there were limitations. Grouping everyone into just three orders was often too general to be of practical value. A wealthy merchant, for example, though clearly a member of the third order, would have been incensed to find himself described as a *laborator* in a legal document. There were grades in the other orders as well. The men of war ranged from the king to the humble knight, lord of a solitary, poverty-stricken manor, who was no better off than many a peasant. The men of prayer ranged from the archbishop to the ignorant, illiterate, half-starved village curate. Divisions between the orders were also blurred. The Bayeux Tapestry shows Bishop Odo charging with the rest of the Norman army at the Battle of Hastings, a *bellator* if ever there was one, his only concession to the rule that a churchman should not shed blood being to carry a large, blunt instrument rather than a sword. Nor was Odo the only battling bishop, by any means. What of the military orders, the Knights Hospitaller and the Knights Templar? Here were men who took much the same vows as monks, yet dedicated themselves to fighting infidels. Also, what of the lay brothers in the Cistercian monasteries? They were monks of a kind, yet they spent their days in manual work. There are many more examples like this, yet, broadly speaking, the division into three orders did hold good.

The clergy were distinct for two reasons. In the first place they were celibate, at least after the papal reforms had taken effect. The morals of some of them might still be suspect, but none of them could be legally married. Secondly, they had all gone through some special form of induction, the priests being ordained and the monks taking the vows required by their religious orders.

The men of war also stood apart for two reasons. The first was that, like the clergy, they had gone through their own ceremony of induction, that of being dubbed knight. This was not true of the early Middle Ages, but, eventually, knighthood became a formal institution to which all the men of war belonged, including kings. Secondly, knights owed their status not only to the ceremony of dubbing but to their birth. Sovereigns could knight or even ennoble commoners, but that did not mean they would be accepted by the older families. Several generations would have to lapse before the taint of humble origins was lost.

Since the clergy and the knights were so well defined, it was easy to identify the people. They were the ones who remained. There were, though, changes to their order. At the time of King Alfred, and for long after it, most of its members were engaged in farming, so they could all be referred to as *rustici, agricultores,* or *laboratores.* Later, though, the towns grew and so did commerce and even industry. The third order spawned its own elite, men of such wealth that they lent money to the king and the aristocracy and who, though they could not change their order, were admitted to the halls of the great and sat at table. They could not be lumped either with the peasants who stank of manure, or with the poverty-stricken day laborers of the city suburbs. Consequently, the men of substance, those who made money in trade and who formed the oligarchies that ran the cities, monopolized the third order. The poor did not form a fourth order. Rather, they were outside the system altogether, in much the same way that the Hindu "untouchables" have no caste.

The threefold classification proved its worth when, in the four-teenth century, the kings of France began to call representative assemblies. Eventually, it became the rule that the national assem-bly, the Estates General, should meet in three houses, clergy, no-bility and third estate. It still had this form when it met in 1789 and, unwittingly, precipitated the French Revolution.

CHAPTER 2
THE FIRST FEUDAL AGE

THE ORIGINS OF FEUDALISM

Feudalism appeared during the Dark Ages, the period of confusion which followed the collapse of the Roman Empire. It survived, more or less intact, until the Renaissance and Reformation, while vestiges of it remained, in some countries at least, until the nineteenth century. It went through many changes, but Marc Bloch in his *Feudal Society* (1939-1940) discerned two main phases which he called the first and second feudal ages. Generally speaking, the transition took place between 1150 and 1200, though the timing varied from country to country.

During the first feudal age the people of Europe lived in comparatively small agricultural communities in the north or the depopulated remnants of Roman cities in the south. Rural villages were well populated, but separated from each other by vast tracts of forests and wastes, like islands scattered over an ocean. There was a certain amount of trade, but it was intermittent and unreliable. Consequently, towns were few and insignificant and there was little money in circulation. Most payments, great or small, had to be made in kind. The peasant might exchange a bag of wheat for a pair of shoes, while a king might reward a faithful retainer with a large estate.

With such a population pattern, and with poor communications, it was difficult for rulers to control their subjects, so that disorders were common. On top of that, there were threats from overseas. Viking raids, which began in the eighth century, were to continue until the eleventh. A French chronicler describes the devastation in France:

7

4. The number of ships increases, the endless flood of Vikings never ceases to grow. Everywhere Christ's people are the victims of massacre, burning and plunder, clear proof of which will remain as long as the world itself endures. The Vikings overrun all that lies before them, and none can withstand them. They seize the cities of Bordeaux, Périgueux, Limoges, Angoulême, Toulouse. Angers, Tours and Orléans are made deserts. The ashes of many a saint are carried away. Thus little by little is coming to pass the prophecy spoken by the Lord through the mouth of His prophet, "Out of the north a scourge shall break forth upon all the inhabitants of the earth."

Ships past counting voyage up the Seine, and throughout the entire region evil grows strong. Rouen is invaded, sacked and set on fire. Paris, Beauvais and Meaux are taken, the fortress of Melun is laid waste, Chartres occupied, Evreux and Bayeux looted, and every town invested. [Ermentarius of Noirmoutier, *Chronicle*]

Sporadic raids were followed by systematic conquest. The Vikings established themselves in Normandy, Ireland, Scotland and much of England. In 1016, the English, despairing of any other remedy, invited a Danish Viking, Canute, to be their king.

While the Vikings were attacking northern Europe, Moors from North Africa were ravaging the Mediterranean countries. Here, too, raids were followed by conquest. The Moors occupied many of the Mediterranean islands, including Sicily, Malta and the Balearics, and, early in the eighth century, they took nearly all of the Iberian Peninsula.

CHAPTER 2. THE FIRST FEUDAL AGE

It was in response to this anarchy that what we know as the "feudal system" evolved. It may have originated with the German tribes who fought against the Romans. The historian Tacitus describes them as they were in his day, that is about A.D. 100:

> 5. They carry out no transactions, public or private, unless they are armed. It is a general rule, though, that no one shall bear arms unless his leaders are satisfied that he is skilled in their use. Then, at a meeting of the tribe, a chief or the youth's father will give him a shield and a spear. These mean the same to the Germans as the toga does to us. They are a public acknowledgment that the youth is no longer just one of a family, but is a citizen in his own right.
>
> Even a boy in his teens can become a chief, if he is of noble birth, or if his father has performed some outstanding service. Such are put in the charge of older men, and none is ashamed to appear as the follower of a chief. There is a hierarchy of rank in these retinues, which is determined by the chief, and men struggle to win the highest place in his esteem. There is also rivalry among the chiefs who seek the honor of having the largest and bravest retinue.
>
> In battle, a chief is disgraced if he is less valiant than his followers, and the followers are disgraced if they are less valiant than their chief. Leaving the battle alive after the death of the chief is to incur lifelong disgrace. All strive to defend and protect him, and allow him to take the credit for their own acts of bravery. The chiefs fight to win the victory, and the followers fight for their chiefs.
>
> If their own country is going through a long period of peace, many noble youths will join other tribes who are at war. For the Germans have no liking for peace; fame is more easily won among dangers, and a leader cannot keep together a large force of retainers without resorting to violence and war.
>
> The followers are constantly demanding favors from their chief, perhaps a war horse, or a spear red with the gore of a

fallen enemy. Their meals, which are copious, though plain, are what they receive instead of pay. The source of all this bounty is war and plunder. A German is not so easily persuaded to till the soil and wait in patience for the harvest, as to defy an enemy, and be rewarded with wounds. He thinks it dull and supine to win slowly by hard work what he can gain quickly at the cost of a little blood. [*Germania*]

HOMAGE

The tribal relationship of chief and follower was to evolve into the feudal relationship of lord and vassal. This development was a complex thread with several strands. One was the taking of oaths of loyalty, the earliest reference to which seems to be an account in a Carolingian chronicle of A.D. 757, describing how Tassilo, duke of Bavaria swore fealty to King Pepin of the Franks. The oath taking became a ceremony of homage. A Flemish chronicler describes one such act, paid to Count William of Flanders in 1127:

6. Homage was done to the count in expression of fealty and loyalty. First, they did their homage thus: the count asked each of them if he wished utterly to become his man, and he answered, "I will," and then the man's joined hands being grasped by the hands of the count, they were bound to one another with a kiss. Secondly, he who had done the homage took an oath of fealty in these words, "I promise on my faith that I will be faithful henceforth to Count William, and that I will keep utterly my homage to him against all

men, in good faith, without guile." And then, in the third place, he confirmed this by swearing an oath on the relics of the saints. Then the count, with a wand in his hand, gave investiture to all who by this compact had promised him loyalty and homage and likewise taken an oath. [Galbert de Bruges, *Deeds of the Count of Flanders*]

FIEFS AND ALLODS

Another feature of the feudal relationship was the conditional grant of land made by the lord to his vassal. The forerunner of this is said to be the *precarium* or benefice, whereby the church surrendered the use of an estate for a period of time, while retaining ownership of it. Precarial grants were first made, it would seem, at the behest of Charles Martel (689-741), who wanted his followers to have the means of supporting themselves. Rulers also granted their vassals benefices, and these became known, eventually, as "fiefs." The following is from a charter granted by a Carolingian king, Charles the Bald, in A.D. 876:

7. Be it known to all men, that our faithful subject, Hildebertus, has beseeched our serenity that we grant him, in right of usufruct and benefice, certain estates which are called Cavaliacus in the county of Limoges. Giving assent to his prayers for reason of his meritorious service, we have ordered this charter to be written, through which we grant to him the estates already mentioned, with lands, vineyards, forests, meadows, pastures, and with the men living upon them so that, without causing any damage through exchanges or diminishing or lessening the land, he for all the days of his life and his son after him, may hold and possess them in right of benefice and usufruct. [*Acts of Charles II, the Bald, King of France*]

At first, most fiefs appear to have been granted for a limited period, usually during the life and good behavior of the vassal. After that, they reverted to the lord. Eventually, though, fiefs became hereditary. The charter of Charles the Bald already quoted grants the fief to both the vassal and his son. Rulers also understood that if they were to maintain the morale and keep the loyalty of their vassals, then they would have to make provision for their heirs. When he was besieging Milan in 1037, Emperor Conrad II made an edict protecting his Italian vassals' rights over their fiefs. It contained the following:

> 8. We command that when a vassal, great or petty, should die, his son shall receive his fief. If he has no son, but is survived by a grandson born of male issue, the grandson should in equal manner have the fief, while respecting the customs of the greater knights in giving horses and arms to their lords. If he does not have a grandson born from male issue and if he should have a legitimate brother from the side of his father, and if that brother, after offending the lord, is willing to make amends, and become his vassal, he should have the fief which was his father's. [*Constitutions of Conrad II*]

Not all estates were fiefs. Many were allods, which meant that those who held them owned them outright. Fiefs could become allods, if their lords relaxed their grip. Equally, allods could become fiefs, as lesser men sought the protection of greater, and this tendency was the more common. But allods survived in France and there were a great many in Germany. In England, however, there were none, because of the Norman Conquest of a.d. 1066. William I rewarded his followers with fiefs and the Crown remained the ultimate owner of all land as, in theory, it still is.

SERVICES

A vassal might owe his lord menial services, such as supporting his head on a sea voyage. In the heat of battle, he would be expected to abandon his own horse, if his lord had need of it. The most common duty for a vassal, though, was to fight, at his own expense, in the lord's army. The laws of the Carolingian kings stated,

CHAPTER 2. THE FIRST FEUDAL AGE

"We wish that the vassal should go with his lord's army and perform his services, in whatever kingdom he should be."

The nature of this military service was significant. In the history of war, the advantage has sometimes been with cavalry and sometimes with infantry. It was infantry legions that conquered and held the Roman Empire, but in the later years of the Empire, cavalry was growing in importance. Then, early in the eighth century, European horsemen adopted the stirrup. This insignificant bit of metal revolutionized warfare, since it allowed the mounted soldier to deliver a hard blow, without the risk of unseating himself. Cavalry now dominated the battle field, so that when a lord summoned his followers to war, he expected them to come mounted, that is to say, he required them to perform "knight service." Mounted knights were as much a part of the feudal age as cowboys were of the Wild West.

Knight service was no small undertaking, for the cost of a suit of armor and a war-horse was considerable, while maintaining a knight in the field was the work of at least five men. A wealthy vassal would have to supply several knights. However, even more was demanded. Fulbert, bishop of Chartres, describes the duties of a vassal:

9. He who takes the oath of fealty to his lord ought always to keep in mind these six things: what is harmless, safe, honorable, useful, easy and practicable. Harmless, which means that he ought not to injure his lord in his body; safe, that he should not injure him by betraying his confidence or the defenses upon which he depends for security; honorable, that he should not injure him in his justice, or in other matters that relate to his honor; useful, that he should not injure him in his property; easy, that he should not make

difficult that which his lord can do easily; and practicable, that he should not make impossible for the lord that which is possible.

However, while it is proper that the faithful vassal should avoid these injuries, it is not for doing this alone that he deserves his fief: for it is not enough to refrain from wrong-doing, unless that which is good is done also. It remains, therefore, that in the same six things referred to above he should faithfully advise and aid his lord, if he wishes to be regarded as worthy of his fief and to be safe concerning the fealty which he has sworn. [*Letter to William, Duke of Aquitaine*, 1020]

The lord, too, had obligations. It was his duty to support his vassal, who had paid homage in the hope of securing such assistance. Bishop Fulbert said that a lord who failed his vassal deserved censure for breach of faith. Jean de Marmoutier describes how, in 960, Count Geoffrey of Anjou disposed of a menace. The story is probably apocryphal, but it shows the spirit that a lord was expected to display:

10. Ethelulf the Dane came near Paris, and offered single combat to any French knight. When he had defeated and killed several of the noblest and bravest of the French, the king was stricken with grief and forbade anyone to fight with Ethelulf. But when Count Geoffrey heard of the Dane's prowess and cruelty, he set off secretly, with a few follow-ers. When he saw the Dane, and heard his war cry, the count himself bellowed and went alone to meet his enemy. Each man spurred his horse and charged. The count's spear pierced the Dane's chest, so that it threw him to the ground with the blade coming out between his shoulders. Even so, the Dane struggled to rise, hate glinting in his eyes. Geoffrey dismounted and, with his sword, cut off his head. He then remounted and rode off, bearing the head and leading his enemy's horse. [*Chronicle of the Counts of Anjou*]

14

CHAPTER 2. THE FIRST FEUDAL AGE

FEUDALISM AND PUBLIC ORDER

The first feudal age saw a heroic attempt to establish some sort of authority over much of Europe. Charles the Great, otherwise known as Charlemagne, revived the title of Roman Emperor and had himself crowned at Rome by Pope Leo III on Christmas Day A.D. 800. But his empire collapsed following his death in 814. Nithard, a member of the court, describes what happened:

11. Louis, known as "the Pious," was the youngest of Charlemagne's legitimate sons, and came to the throne after all the others had died. At the beginning of his reign he divided his father's huge treasure into three. One part paid for the funeral. The other two parts he shared with those of his sisters who were legitimate. He also ordered his sisters to leave court immediately and go into nunneries. His illegitimate brothers Drogo, Hugo and Theodoric, were still very young, and he gave orders that they should be brought up in the court. He gave the kingdom of Italy to his nephew, Bernard, who was Pepin's son. But Bernard turned against Louis and he was first blinded, then killed by Bertmund, the governor of Lyons. After that, Louis feared that his other brothers might also turn against him, so he summoned them before his council, tonsured them and sent them to monasteries.

When this had been done, he made his sons marry and divided the empire between them. Pepin was given Aquitaine, Louis had Bavaria while Lothair was to have the whole empire after his father's death. Meanwhile, their mother, Queen Irmengardis, had died, and soon afterwards, Louis married Judith, who gave birth to Charles.

Louis did not know what he could do for Charles, since he had divided his empire between his other sons. He could only plead with them, and Lothair finally agreed that he would give Charles whatever part of the kingdom he wanted. He also swore an oath that he would be Charles's protector and defend him against his enemies. But led on by his father-in-law and others, he soon regretted what he had done and tried to undermine all the arrangements Louis had made. To defeat these plots, Louis made Bernard, duke of Septimania, his chamberlain, giving him the care of Charles and entrusting him with the administration of the empire. Bernard, though, abused this trust and weakened the imperial authority.

Eventually, Charles was given Alamannia, and Lothair had the pretext he needed. He called on his brothers and the people to restore the empire to order. They descended on Louis at Compiègne, made the queen enter a nunnery and sent her brothers to Aquitaine, where they were held by Pepin. Bernard fled to Septimania, but his brother Herbert was taken, blinded and imprisoned. Lothair now assumed the government of the empire, keeping his father and Charles in confinement. Charles was handed to monks, who were told to accustom him to the life of the monastery and persuade him to become a monk himself. [Nithard, *Histories*]

That was by no means the end of the conflict. The brothers quarreled amongst themselves and the redoubtable Judith, Charles's mother, entered the fray. Louis the Pious died in 840, after which there were three years of strife. Then, the empire was partitioned by the Treaty of Verdun.

There were, as well, many local conflicts, since feudalism had created numerous semi-autonomous armed bands. For example, in 987 when Fulk Nerra became Count of Anjou, he was only seventeen, and some of his leading nobles decided to take advantage of his youth to rebel against him. Fulk met his enemies at Châteaudun:

12. The people of the town attacked the count's men. The Angevins kept them at bay until evening, but when they tried to retreat, they found themselves cut off by the men of Châteaudun, who were assailing them in the rear. Seeing there was no escape, the Angevins returned to the fight. They attacked on every front, and surrounded and defeated their foes. The men of Châteaudun fled, but the battle continued, with

the count pursuing them into their camp, capturing many and slaughtering others. That night, the Angevins rested in the place, guarding two hundred knights they had captured and bound, along with other prisoners. The next day, they plundered the countryside all around, bringing ruin to its people. Drunk with success, they then returned to Amboise.

[Jean de Marmoutier, *Chronicles of the Counts of Anjou*]

The lesser knights were particularly capable, for example, of riding full tilt through a peasant's crops in the summer and then demanding fodder from him in the fall. It was easy to build castles which were no more than mounds of earth topped with wooden defenses and, given that siege tactics were still primitive, such castles made comparatively safe refuges from which to terrorize the surrounding countryside. That was what happened in 1121 when a certain Stephen de Varenne fell out with the abbey of Savigny, near Lyons, in France:

13. The same Stephen made a fortification out of a house which his father had built at a distance of one league from the abbey. He enclosed it with a mound and a moat, fortified it with wooden towers and stockades, and began to force the serfs of the abbey by threats and tortures to do service to him. Distraught by these injuries, Abbot Ponce admonished his vassal Stephen that he should come to trial. For long he contemptuously refused. Upon the counsel of his friends, however, he gave hostages. The trial was set in the court of the abbot. The judges, after hearing both sides, gave this judgment. Stephen ought to return the fortification to the abbot, who could destroy as much of it as he pleased. In the churchyard, between his church and the house, he should allow a passage to the chaplains of the church. For a long time Stephen delayed complying with this judgment and did not surrender the fortress to the abbot. But when the abbot started to open a path through the churchyard, Stephen with an armed band assaulted the monks who were there, hurling at them both missiles and insulting words. Then, upon

17

leaving, he came to his fortress and threw out the guards of the abbot who were there. He did not cease ravaging the lands of the abbey. Among other ills, he invaded a cell in which six monks were permanently residing. He arrogantly expelled the monks and destroyed their possessions. [*Cartulary of the Abbey of Savigny*]

SUCH, THEN, in broad outline, was the feudal system. There was the association of like-minded, mounted warriors, imbued with much the same spirit as was shown by the German tribes of the time of Tacitus; there was the emergence of lords and vassals, who replaced chiefs and followers; there was the taking of oaths of fealty by the ceremony of homage; there was the conditional grant of estates, which became known as fiefs; there was knight service, given in exchange for those fiefs; there was the tendency for fiefs to become hereditary; there were codes of conduct governing the mutual responsibilities of lords and vassals.

This view of feudalism has been simplified in the interests of brevity and clarity, so it is necessary to sound a few notes of caution. It should not be imagined that the feudal system was at all clearly defined. In her *Fiefs and Vassals,* published in 1994, Susan Reynolds makes a sweeping attack on the traditional view of feudalism. She points out, among other things, that there were no coherent land laws but rather a tangled undergrowth of customary law, that homage meant "different things to different people at different times," that there were "vassals without fiefs and fiefs without vassals," and that the contrast between allod and fief was "more variable" than has been suggested. Ms. Reynolds's book, however, is flawed in that it is far too negative. Having demolished, as she thinks, the traditional view of feudalism and failed to put anything coherent in its place, she concludes her book with the remark, "I have no wish to create a new model into which evidence is to be fitted as it has been fitted for centuries into the model of feudalism." But in history, as in automobile engineering, it is unwise to consign the old model to the scrap yard before a new one is in production. The old vehicle may be less than perfect, but it has given good service and will continue to do so, until something better makes an appearance. Similarly, most students will find the traditional model of feudalism useful and, though bearing Ms. Reynolds's caveats in mind, would be ill-advised to discard it entirely until someone has produced a superior version.

CHAPTER 3
THE SECOND FEUDAL AGE

DURING THE FIRST FEUDAL AGE, as we have seen, central government was weak, so that nobles and knights behaved much as they pleased. During the second feudal age, the tables were turned, at least in some countries. Here, feudal institutions, so far from allowing disruption, became the instruments which kings used to control their subjects.

The eleventh and twelfth centuries saw important changes. Europeans, who had been the victims for so long, went over to the attack and pushed back their frontiers. The Germans began their march to the east, which was to continue until the Second World War. In the south, lands were reconquered from the Moors, including Sicily and much of the Iberian Peninsula. At the same time, the population of Europe grew, the wastes were colonized and communities lost much of their isolation. Trade increased, so that the towns grew in size and importance. Merchants were both wealthier and more numerous. There was far more money in circulation.

All these changes benefited rulers. Success in war gave them prestige and there were new sources of wealth they could tap. Moreover, they collected those revenues in coin. If a ruler is paid his dues in fodder, he can only feed it to his horses, but if he is paid in coin, he can put it to a multitude of uses.

ADMINISTRATION

One way that rulers spent their money was in establishing government departments, staffed by paid bureaucrats. The English exchequer, which first appeared early in the twelfth century, is a good example. It had two divisions, the lower exchequer which received the king's revenues and the higher exchequer, which was a court of law that settled disputes. The exchequer took its name from the chequered board which the clerks used for their calculations. They needed this aid, since doing arithmetic with Roman numerals caused hideous problems, one them being that there is no Roman symbol for zero.

In about 1177 Richard Fitzneal, bishop of London, wrote his remarkable *Dialogue of the Exchequer,* an imaginary conversation in which an old hand, the Master, explains the workings of the department to a novice. This extract is from the preface:

> 14. We must all subject ourselves to the powers appointed by God, "For there is no power but of God." Therefore it does not seem foolish or wrong for churchmen to uphold the authority of kings by serving them. Kings should not only be served by displaying the glory of their authority, but also in ensuring the abundance of wealth to which their position entitles them. The one may secure glory, but it is the other which gives support. It follows that ample or insufficient funds can raise or lower the standing of princes. Those who lack wealth fall prey to their enemies, but when they have wealth, their enemies fall prey to them.

CHAPTER 3. THE SECOND FEUDAL AGE

It is true that kings sometimes gain wealth unjustly and by force, but it is not for their subjects to discuss or condemn them. The hearts of kings are controlled by God, and those whom God has entrusted with the care of the people should be subject to divine, not human, judgment. Therefore, no matter how the wealth is acquired, those charged with its administration must not waver in their duty. Rather, in collecting, saving and spending they should display care and diligence, as if they were to answer for the security of the kingdom, which this wealth guarantees.

Of course, we know full well that kingdoms must be ruled with prudence, fortitude, temperance, justice and many other virtues, and rulers must do all they can to cultivate these virtues. But it sometimes happens that good advice and sound intelligence may suggest a course of action which can be followed more quickly with the help of money. Also, what seems to be difficult is often easily achieved with money, as if it had some special skill in solving problems.

Money is needed not only in time of war, but also in time of peace. It can be spent fortifying cities, paying salaries and in many other ways to preserve the realm. Although there is no war, devout rulers who have money can build churches, feed and clothe the poor, and distribute wealth in other charitable works. [*Dialogue of the Exchequer*]

Here the Master explains the origins and importance of money rents:

15. As our fathers have told us, after the Conquest kings received neither gold nor silver from their manors, but only payments in kind. These payments provided the royal household with its daily needs, and the servants who collected them knew what was due from each manor. But for wages and gifts to knights, the king needed coined money, which came from the profits of his law courts and from the towns. This went on throughout the reign of William I and until the reign of his son, King Henry. Even I knew men who had

seen the payments in kind carried from the royal manors to the court. The officers of the royal household had a detailed knowledge of those counties from which wheat was due, or different kinds of meat, or fodder for horses, and other needful supplies. When the payments were made, the royal officials gave the sheriffs receipts for the goods, by stating their value in money. Thus a quantity of wheat that would make bread for a hundred men was valued at one shilling; for an ox, one shilling; for a ram or a sheep, four pennies; for enough fodder for twenty horses, also one shilling.

But later, when the king was fighting overseas, he had to have coined money, if he was to carry out his plans. Meanwhile, mobs of peasants gathered at the king's court to protest, and, what upset him even more, they met him at the roadside, holding aloft their plowshares, symbolizing the ruin of their farms. They suffered badly, for they had to carry their payments in kind to many parts of the realm. The king heard their complaints, and, on the advice of his barons, sent prudent, discreet men to investigate. These men surveyed the royal manors in person, and they estimated the value, in money, of the payments in kind that were due from them. They then totaled the amounts due from each county and made the sheriffs responsible for paying them to the Exchequer. [Ibid.]

Money also solved a problem connected with knight service:

16. The King to the Sheriff of York, greeting.

Though we lately commanded you that you should summon archbishops, bishops, abbots, priors and other ecclesiastical persons, and also widows and other women who hold of us in chief by knight service, that they should have at our side on the feast of Whitsuntide next coming, at Berwick-on-Tweed, their whole service due to us, well furnished with horses and arms and ready to march against the Scots, our enemies; wishing, however, to spare the labors of the same bishops, religious persons, women and others, who are

unskilled or even unfit for arms, we command you to proclaim that they may make fine with us for their service, to
wit £20 for a knight's fee, or else they must be at our side on
the feast of Whitsunday as they are bound.

Witness the King at Laneham, 16 April. [*Patent Roll,
Edward I, 1303*]

Eventually, it became general to pay a tax known as "scutage,"
or "shield money," instead of giving knight service. Those who
wanted to fight could still do so, but the rest were spared. The
king also enjoyed advantages. Knight service was, normally, for
forty days a year, and when their time was up, men went home.
Scutage, though, allowed the king to enlist an army of professional
soldiers, which was much more efficient than the undisciplined
feudal levy. This is one explanation for the success of the English
armies in France during the Hundred Years War.

ENFORCEMENT OF FEUDAL RIGHTS: ENGLAND

The following documents show how the kings of England used
their officials to collect information and enforce their feudal rights.

Here is a survey made on the death of a vassal. A jury of twelve
gave evidence to the king's escheator [the official responsible for
estates that have lapsed to the crown]:

17. Hugh Poyntz held the manor of Curry Mallet by the service of one knight's fee. In this manor is a capital messuage
[house] which is worth 4s-0d a year with the fruit and herb-
age of the garden. And there are 280 acres of arable land
which is worth £4-13s-4d a year at 4d an acre. And there are
60 acres of meadow which are worth £4-10s-0d a year at 18d
an acre. And there is a park which is worth 6s-8d a year and
not more owing to the keeping of deer. And the fines from
the court are worth 4s-0d a year. And there are 12 free tenants who pay yearly at the feasts of Michaelmas and Easter
by equal portions 74s-8d. And there are 16 customary tenants, each of whom holds half a virgate in villeinage, and

the works of each are worth 2s-od a year. And there are 28 customary tenants each of which holds half a virgate of land in villeinage, paying yearly 2s-od and the works of each are worth 12d. Total sum £22-12s-8d. [*Inquisition post mortem*, Edward II, 1308]

The correct total is £19-8s-8d. The mistake was perhaps the result of doing the calculations in Roman numerals.

A fief reverted to the king on the death of one of his vassals, though it was usual for the vassal's heir to take over the fief, doing homage for it and, perhaps, paying a fine:

18. The King to Simon Beresford, his escheator;

We have heard from you that Nichola, the widow of Nicholas de Mortesthorp, held on the day she died the manor of Kingston Russell, and the manor is held of us in chief by the service of counting our chessmen and of putting them in a box when we have finished our game. And that Nichola also held the manor of Allington by knight service. And that Theobald Russell is the heir of the manors. We have taken Theobald's homage for the manors and have given them back to him. And therefore we command you to cause the same Theobald to have full possession of the manors aforesaid.

Witness the King at Gloucester. [*Fine Roll*, Edward III, 1329]

When a woman inherited, it was usual for her husband to perform her knight service for her, so the king was anxious that an heiress should marry someone he found congenial. If the woman wed without a royal license, she and her husband could be in trouble:

19. The King to his beloved and trusty escheator, greeting.

Whereas Millicent, widow of Hugh de Plesey, took an oath that she would not marry without our license, has now married Richard de Stanley without our license. We, refusing to pass over such a contempt unpunished, command you that you take into our hand all the lands which the aforesaid Richard and Millicent hold in Millicent's dower of inheritance of the aforesaid Hugh. [*Fine Roll*, Edward I, 1273]

Men's marriages were also controlled:

20. To all faithful who shall see or hear these presents, Robert de Reydon, knight, greeting in the Lord.

Whereas the marriage of Robert, son and heir of Robert Maukel, belongs to me by reason of certain lands which he holds of me by knight service, and whereas the said Robert, without my license or will, hath married himself to Joan, daughter of Thomas Stace of Ipswich; know that I have pardoned the said Thomas Stace and the said Robert, for 20 marks of silver which they have given me. [*Harleian Manuscripts*, British Museum, 1312]

Heirs who were minors became the king's wards. He would protect, maintain and educate them, but he took the income from their fiefs and married them to whom he pleased. Wardship became a useful source of income for the Crown:

21. The King to his beloved and trusty William Trussel, his escheator, greeting.

We command you that you cause the body of the heir of Roger de Huntingfield deceased, who held of us in chief, wheresoever it be found, to be seized into our hand and to be sent to us without delay. [*Fine Roll*, Edward II, 1337]

22. By fine of £6 which our beloved clerk, Adam de Lymbergh has made with us, we have granted to him the marriage of John, son and heir of Joan de Chodewell, deceased, who held of us in chief, which John is under age and in our wardship to hold without disparagement.

And command is given to Richard de Rodenay, the king's escheator, that he deliver to the same Adam the body of the heir aforesaid, to be married in the form aforesaid. [*Fine Roll*, Edward II, 1320]

23. Greetings and affectionate regards.

My lord, we have learned that the Foliot marriage concerns a demoiselle, wherefore we consider the thing more noble and rich than we had thought. We therefore beg you my lord, that for the profit of our lord the king, you cause the said demoiselle to be seized, and put in good ward, so that the lord king may profit thereby. For you know that the wardship of a woman is often perilous, and there is danger that our lord the king may not profit because she is not in hand. [Chancery Warrants, 1325. *Letter from chancellor to sheriff*]

In fact, there were two heiresses, Margery and Margaret Foliot, for whose marriages the king had £200 each. Margery was kept by the constable of the Tower of London until handed over, for £200, to Isabel de Hastyng.

Wrecks were usually the property of the king:

24. The King to the sheriff of Kent, greeting.

We understand that a great mass of a whale lately cast ashore by the coast of the River Thames, which should belong to us as our wreck, and a great part of which has been carried away by certain evil-doers, remains still in your keeping. We order you that you cause all of the whale aforesaid to be delivered without delay to our beloved and trusty Nicholas de la Beche, constable of our Tower of London. [*Fine Roll*, Edward III, 1337]

ENFORCEMENT OF FEUDAL RIGHTS: SICILY

Another country that acquired a strong monarchy was Sicily. Like many of the Mediterranean lands, it had been conquered by the Moors. But Norman adventurers established themselves in southern Italy and, in 1061, a band of them led by Roger de Hauteville landed in Sicily. By 1091 the Normans were masters of the whole of the island. Later, Roger II (1101-1154) welded the Norman territories of southern Italy and Sicily into a united kingdom, establishing his authority over the Greeks, Lombards, Moors and Normans that inhabited it. He appointed justiciars to control local government and, in 1140, issued a code of laws known as the *Assizes of Ariano*.

CHAPTER 3. THE SECOND FEUDAL AGE

In 1198 a German prince, Frederick of Hohenstaufen, inherited Sicily, but he was only a child of four. The royal authority collapsed as nobles, bishops, abbots, towns and foreign merchants all seized privileges for themselves. When he reached his majority, Frederick's first concern was to become Roman Emperor, as his father had been. He was elected in 1220, becoming the Emperor Frederick II. From 1228-1229 he was on a crusade. Meanwhile, he had quarreled with the pope, who took advantage of his absence to invade southern Italy. Frederick returned, expelled the papal armies and then restored order in his kingdom.

Frederick consolidated his military success by issuing a remarkable code of royal laws known at the *Constitutions of Melfi*. The lawyers who did the work for him drew on the customary laws of the Normans, Greeks and Lombards, Canon Law, Roman Law and existing royal laws. There were no major innovations and many local customs remained, but there was now a coherent body of law to regulate important matters throughout the realm.

The *Constitutions of Melfi* show how a wise and powerful ruler governed a feudal kingdom. The first essential was that the nobles should be tamed:

25. TITLE IX. ABOUT THOSE WHO INCITE WAR IN THE KINGDOM AND HOW ATTACKS SHOULD BE PUNISHED

> A count, baron, knight, or anyone else who publicly incites war in the kingdom should suffer death and the confiscation of all his goods. Moreover, whoever makes attacks or counterattacks should be punished by the confiscation of half his goods.

TITLE X. ABOUT THE ILLEGAL BEARING OF ARMS AND THE PUNISHMENT FOR STRIKING WITH THEM

> We not only wish to punish crimes that have been committed, but also to prevent the occasion for them arising. Therefore, since bearing illegal arms sometimes causes strife and murder, we choose to prevent it now rather than punish it later. By this law, we order that none of our subjects shall carry sharpened and forbidden weapons, such as small knives with points, swords, lances, breast plates, shields or suits of

mail, maces, or any others which are designed to cause injury, rather than for some lawful use.

However, we allow judges and their servants to carry such forbidden weapons as long as they are with us in our court, or are going to and from their homes, or are journeying on our business. We also exempt knights, the sons of knights and townsmen from this law. We do not forbid them to carry swords when they travel outside the area in which they live. But when they have returned to their areas, or are the guests of others, they should put away their swords at once.

Further, whoever carries illegal weapons shall pay our treasury five ounces of gold if he is a count, four ounces if he is a baron, three ounces if he is an ordinary knight and one ounce if he is a peasant.

The master justiciar [chief justice] and the justiciars are to deal justly with all these cases.

TITLE XLIX. NO PRELATE, COUNT, OR BARON MUST HOLD THE OFFICE OF JUSTICIAR

We desire that none should presume to usurp those powers which are our own special prerogative. Therefore by this decree, which shall be in force for ever, we expressly forbid bishops, counts, barons and knights to dare to exercise the office of justiciar in their own lands or to delegate it to anyone else. Rather, they should obey the master justiciar and the justiciars established by our authority. Those who defy this edict shall by punished by the confiscation of their lands.

TITLE XX. WHEN AIDS MAY BE LEVIED

Our subjects often complain because bishops, counts, barons, and knights levy aids whenever it suits them. Therefore, since we wish to prevent the cruel oppression of our subjects, we order that lords may levy an aid only in the following cases: for the ransom of the lord, if he is captured by our enemies while in our service, for making his son a knight; for buying land, but only once and only when he buys it to serve us in our army; and a reasonable amount for our keep when we are their guests in their lands or should need support from them. In all these cases, however, lords should levy only a moderate aid.

TITLE XXXII. ABOUT NEW CONSTRUCTION

We order that castles, fortifications and towers built after the death of our cousin, King William, of blessed memory, must be demolished. Those who refuse to destroy these fortifications before the Feast of the Nativity of the Lord next coming shall be punished by the confiscation of all their goods. We also enact that no one shall build fortifications without our permission.

Frederick was also concerned that fiefs should continue to provide him with the services which were his due, That meant that the fiefs should remain intact and not fall into the wrong hands:

TITLE V. ON FIEFS

We decree that all conveyances and agreements which diminish or change fiefs shall be completely invalid, unless they have our special permission.

We forbid all our subjects, counts, barons, knights, or any other person or churchman, to dare to convey [title to] property from which rents or services are due to us, by any process of any kind, whether they are still living, or in their wills, or to change it in such a manner so that we lose the same rent or service.

TITLE XV. ON DOWRIES

We allow a baron or a knight to establish a dowry, if he holds two fiefs, and if he has only one and a half fiefs, he may establish a dowry of half a fief. But if he has only one fief, he may establish a dowry only in money and not in land.

TITLE XVI. ON THE ESTABLISHMENT OF DOWRIES

On the death of her husband, a woman who has a dower in land must swear fealty for that dower to the heir. She must also promise that she will not seek by devious means to separate her dower from the estate.

TITLE XXIII. A WOMAN MUST NOT BE MARRIED WITHOUT ROYAL
PERMISSION

So that we may maintain the dignity of our crown, we decree that no count, baron, knight or anyone else who holds
from us in chief shall dare to marry without our license.
They must not marry off their daughters, sisters, grand-
daughters, or any other girls for whom they may arrange
marriages, nor may they marry off their sons, giving them
goods or lands.

TITLE XXIV. ON THE SUCCESSION OF NOBLES TO FIEFS

When a count or baron has taken the road of all flesh, their
sons or grandsons must not dare to accept homage from
their vassals until they have received our permission. All who
disobey will suffer confiscation of their goods and lands.

Frederick, however, wished to govern through and with the feudal system. He had no plans to dismantle it:

TITLE XVIII. ON VASSALS' PROMISES OF FEALTY TO THEIR LORDS

Vassals should promise fealty to their lords on life, limb,
capture and worldly honor. They must not reveal any advice that they may give them. If they hear any evil about
their lords which they cannot contradict themselves, they
must inform their lords of it as soon as possible. They must
not act in any way which would cause them to lose the lands
which they hold from their lords. Instead, they must defend
their lords as best they can, saving only their loyalty and
obedience to us and to our heirs.

TITLE XIX. ABOUT PLEDGES

If a vassal refuses to give a pledge for his lord, or if he commits a crime against him, his children or his wife, or will not
support him in court when others bring charges against him,
then the lord may deprive him of his fief, by judgment in
his own court.

If a lord refuses to give a pledge for a vassal who is accused of a crime, or if he beats him without reason, or if he

commits adultery with his wife, or rapes his daughter, then the man is freed from his homage, and is subjected directly to us.

Frederick also recognized that knights and nobles enjoyed special privileges and status:

TITLE XLVII. HOW THE HONOR OF COUNTS, BARONS, AND KNIGHTS SHOULD BE PRESERVED.

So that the honor of every nobleman in our kingdom may be preserved, counts, barons and other knights are to be judged by their peers. Whether they are accused of crimes, or sued in a civil case, they must not be judged save by counts, barons, and those who hold their fiefs directly from us. The sentences should be decided with the judgment of honest men and on the advice of other nobles, and in consultation with our judges. Even if they are not all present throughout the hearing, the justiciars and judges should, none the less, give a thorough explanation of the case and have full discussions with the nobles who pass sentence. By these means, the counts and barons should take care to conclude the case according to the laws of God, of justice and our sacred decrees. If these are not appropriate, then they should be guided by the accepted customs of the kingdom, or by the common laws, provided that such customs and laws do not conflict with our decrees or those of our predecessors.

Should the defendant appeal to our senior judges or to us, the appeal judge, who must also be a count or a baron, should uphold or dismiss the appeal, taking the advice of other counts and barons, judges and honest men.

TITLE CI. ON THE CREDENCE THAT SHOULD BE GIVEN TO NOBLES AND OTHERS IN CASES OF DEBT

We decree that in cases of debt, not only should the amounts be considered, but also the status of the litigants. The oath of a count should alone be sufficient for amounts up to one hundred ounces of gold, a baron should be believed for fifty, an ordinary knight for twenty-five, a townsman of good standing for one pound. The oaths of all others should be accepted for no more than three ounces, no other proof being needed. However, where higher amounts than these are involved, the plaintiff must produce genuine documents or honest witnesses to prove his case.

TITLE XLIII. ON INJURIES TO NOBLES
In order to preserve distinctions of rank, we decree that a townsman or peasant who hits a knight shall be punished by the loss of the hand that delivered the blow, unless he can prove he was defending himself. The son of a nobleman who has not yet been knighted should suffer the same penalty, if he strikes one of higher rank. If a knight strikes a knight, he shall suffer the loss of his horses and weapons and be exiled for a year. If a knight strikes a townsman or a peasant who is not his vassal, the judges should weigh all the facts of the case and make a decision based on the gravity of the injury and on the oath of the victim.

It was not an offense for a knight to strike his own vassals.

It is clear, then, that although Frederick II was determined to assert his prerogatives, he had no intention of overthrowing feudalism in his kingdom. He owed his strength to the support of loyal barons, so he was obliged to acknowledge the privileges and dignity of the whole order of knighthood. He used feudal institutions to enhance his power, but he could not dispense with them. Indeed, any medieval ruler who tried to govern entirely on his own authority was courting trouble.

THE HOLY ROMAN EMPIRE

It should be stressed that not all monarchies grew in strength during the second feudal age. For example, the ruler with the most grandiose title of all, the Holy Roman Emperor, lost authority rather than gained it. Charlemagne's empire disintegrated after his death, as we have seen, and by the eleventh century the

"Roman" Empire consisted of much of what is now modern Germany, the Rhineland and northern Italy.

The emperors struggled to keep their power, but they met vigorous opposition. The princes not only asserted their independence, but spread chaos by feuding among themselves. The lesser knights emerged as a separate and highly disruptive class. Towns grew in wealth and began to claim independence. In 1180, Frederick I, Barbarossa, did manage to defeat his most "overmighty subject," Henry the Lion, duke of Saxony, but this was an isolated success.

Meanwhile, the emperors were embroiled in Italy, where the cities of Lombardy defied them, often with success. The unknown author of an epic poem describes the problems that faced Frederick I (1155-1190):

26. There was a city famous for its wars.
A lovely city, powerful and rich,
Liguria's capital, it was called Milan.
Her large population burned with love for Mars
And swaggered in the glory of its town.
To consuls, chosen by them every year,
They promised to control the way they lived,
And under these they kept the laws and faith.
Yet sharply they harassed the nearby towns
By pressing them for booty and with war,
And two captured cities were reduced to ruins,
First Lodi and then Como fell.
They compelled obedience from wretched serfs
And heavily oppressed the conquered people,
Who were forbidden to repair their homes.
The rest of Liguria would be conquered next
Because their love for power was so great.
And who can count the tribute and the plunder,
The robberies or the castles smashed to ruins?
Who is able to relate the captives' pain,
Their chains, or their innumerable complaints?
The burghers, peasants, and the men who held

The citadels and the sloping hills were frightened.
Not otherwise the herd flees through the woods
The lion and his quickly moving jaws.
There were no people who would dare begin
An open war against Milan. For fear
Had conquered all, and victory made her bold.
The furies and the passion to do harm
Inflamed the spirits of the nearby towns,
And those who sought to give each other help
Preferred to start an internecine war.
Wild Brescia bit Bergamo; Piacenza
And Cremona struck at Parma. Mantua
Was fearful of Verona, and Tortona
Of Pavia, and Pavia of Milan.
Since the rule of law was broken, all bore arms,
And the local cities ripped each others throats.
With their minds corrupted people went insane,
Nor could the fear of God or the restraint
Of law prevent the oppression of the weak.
Just so the horse that feels himself more able
Wants to dominate the grassy meadow.
He neighs and he attacks, now here now there,
To wound his rivals with his hoofs or teeth.
Without protection no poor man was safe.
Nor were travelers secure from all the thieves.
Fraud, robbery and deceit reigned everywhere.
Such was the state of Italy and Liguria.
[*Barbarossa in Italy*, ll. 6-54]

Moreover, pope and emperor were in conflict from time to time.
The pope frequently gained the upper hand as, for example, in
1077, when Gregory II compelled Henry IV to make humble submission to him at Canossa. This following extract from a bull that
Innocent IV issued against Frederick II shows the high claims the
pope made:

27. Whoever tries to undermine the authority of the Vicar of Christ, defies the authority of Christ himself. The King of Kings has given us a mandate over the whole world, attributing to us the full power conceded to the prince of the apostles, and giving us the authority to bind or loosen whoever and whatever may be. The Roman pontiff may exercise his power over any Christian, and especially when there is the guilt of sin. Temporal powers may not be exercised outside the church, since God has created no power outside her.

They lack wisdom and know not how to trace matters to their origins, those who imagine that the apostolic see received imperial sovereignty from Constantine, who held it in former times. Our Lord Jesus Christ, son of God, true man and true God, true king and true priest, has constituted for the benefit of the Holy See a monarchy which is not only pontifical, but royal. He has given to the Blessed Peter and to his successors the reins of empire, both terrestrial and heavenly, as is shown by his several keys. The Vicar of Christ has received the power to exercise jurisdiction, on the one hand over the earth in temporal matters, and on the other hand, over heaven in spiritual matters. [Bull *Eger Cui Levia*, 1245]

The emperor's absences in Italy were opportunities for the German princes to assert themselves. Frederick ii, who was as jealous of his authority as any ruler, took a realistic view of Germany. He even granted more independence to the German princes so that they would be quiet while he pursued other aims, such as consolidating his hold on Sicily.

In 1254, the title "Holy" was added to that of "Roman" emperor. It is significant that the office of Holy Roman Emperor never became hereditary. Instead, when an emperor died, a group of the more powerful princes elected his successor. Emperor Charles iv formalized the system in his Golden Bull of 1356, which nominated seven electors, three of them archbishops and four secular princes. In the fifteenth century, the Hapsburgs became hereditary emperors in fact, if not in law, but by then the empire had fragmented

completely. There were more than thirty powerful secular princi-
palities, ninety ecclesiastical ones, too many minor lordships to
count and numerous free cities.

CHAPTER 4
THE KING

ROYAL AUTHORITY

In countries with a strong monarchy, the king was the leader of the feudal host, whose members had paid him homage. But homage was a contract between free men, and had the king depended on that alone, he would have been no more than first among his equals. A monarch, though, had mystical and even divine attributes. According to legend, the lilies of France appeared miraculously on the shield of Clovis, king of the Franks (481-511), leading to his victory at Tolbiac and his conversion to Christianity in 496. These accounts describe the coronation of Charlemagne in 800:

> 28. It seemed to Pope Leo and all the holy fathers, and to the rest of the Christian people, that they ought to name Charles, king of the Franks, as emperor, seeing that he held Rome itself, where the Caesars had been wont to have their seat, and that he had also the other seats which he held in Italy and Gaul, and also in Germany; for since God Almighty had granted that all these seats should be in his power, it seemed therefore just in their eyes that he should also have the name, with the aid of God and according to the petition of all the Christian people. Whose petition King Charles was unwilling to refuse, but, being subject to God in all humility, on the petition of the priests and all the Christian people he took the name of emperor on the day of the Nativity of our Lord Jesus Christ, and was consecrated by the Lord Pope Leo. [*Annales Laureshamenses*]

> 29. At the coming of the day of the Nativity of Our Lord Jesus Christ, in the church of St. Peter the Apostle, all were assembled

together, and thereupon the venerable and gracious pope crowned him with his own hands with a most precious crown. Then all the faithful in Rome, seeing the great care and love which he bore to the holy Roman Church and its vicar, cried together in a loud voice, by the will of God and St. Peter, the bearer of the keys of the kingdom of heaven, "Life and victory to Charles the most pious Augustus crowned by God, the great and peacemaking emperor." Before the holy tomb of St. Peter the apostle, with the invocation of many saints, this was done thrice; and he was made by all the emperor of the Romans. [*Liber Pontificialis*]

The following comes from a code of laws issued by Alfonso the Wise, king of Castile and Leon (1252-1284), in about 1254:

30. What is a king? Kings are the vicars of God, each one in his kingdom, placed over the people to keep them in the paths of justice and truth, in this world, even as the emperor in his empire. This is manifested in two ways. The first is spiritual, as is shown by the prophets and the saints, to whom Our Lord gave the grace to know things certainly and to make them understood. The second is according to nature, as has been shown by those wise men who have deep knowledge of the world of nature.

The saints said that the king is placed on earth as the representative of God, to administer justice and to give to everyone his due. And because of that, he is called the heart and the soul of the people. For as the soul dwells in the heart of man, and gives life to the body, and supports it, so justice dwells in the king, who is the life and sustenance of his realm. And, moreover, as the heart is one, and keeps all the members in harmony to make one body, so all the people of the kingdom, though they be many, because the king is one, must all be at one with him, to serve him and help him in the things that he must do.

And in accordance with nature, the wise men said that the king is the head of the kingdom. As the thoughts which come

40

from the head direct all the body, so the commands which come from the king, who is the lord and head of all his kingdom, direct the people, who must be ordered and guided by him, and be in harmony with him, to obey him, and protect and increase the kingdom; of which he is the soul and the head, and they the members. [*Siete Partidas*]

The great Florentine poet, Dante (1265-1321), wrote:

31. The temporal monarchy is necessary for the good of the world. This proposal, to which there can be no objection, either on the grounds of reason or authority, may be demonstrated with sound and very clear arguments, above all by the Philosopher [Aristotle] in his *Politics*. He affirms that when various causes are directed to one end, it is best that one person should rule and govern and that the rest should be ruled and guided. This is credible, not only because of the glorious name of the author, but because right reason shows it to be so.

If we consider a man, we see what happens with him. Since all his efforts are directed towards securing happiness, the force of his intellect regulates and rules the rest of him, in default of which he cannot attain the happiness aforesaid.

If we consider a family, whose purpose is the well being of all its members, it is equally right that there should be one

41

who orders and rules. He is the father of the family, or one who carries out his functions, for, as the Philosopher teaches, "Every household is governed by its oldest member." It is his duty, as Homer says, to guide everyone and make rules for them. This is the origin of the proverbial curse, "May you have an equal in your home."

If we consider a village, whose purpose is to secure the co-operation of all its people and resources, it is right that there should be one who rules the others, whether he be appointed from outside, or risen on account of his own qualities and the agreement of the rest; if the contrary happens, not only is there no mutual assistance, but, in the end, when several seek to prevail, all is debased.

If we consider a city, whose purpose is the life and well being of its inhabitants, it is right that there should be one in control. When anything different happens, not only does civil life fail to achieve its ends, but the city itself ceases to be what it was.

Finally, if we consider a kingdom, whose purpose is the same as a city's, but with greater confidence in its peace, it is also right that there should be a king who reigns and governs. If the contrary happens, not only do the subjects fail to achieve their aims, but the kingdom itself perishes, as the ineffable truth proclaims, "Every divided kingdom shall be laid waste." If then, this happens in all affairs that are directed towards an end, what we have stated at the beginning is true.

Well now: it is certain that the whole human race is directed towards an end, as has already been shown; it follows that there should be one who commands and reigns; and he must be called monarch or emperor. The obvious conclusion is, that for the good of the world, it is needful to have either monarchy or empire. [*On Monarchy*]

The following is the preamble to Frederick II's *Constitutions of Melfi:*

32. When God had made the world, he looked at his work and was pleased. He created man in his own image, a little lower than the angels, and gave him dominion over all other living

creatures. He breathed into him the breath of life and he gave him a wife, taken from his body. He created them immortal, but he gave them a command, and because they refused to obey it, he punished them by making them mortal. But so that his earlier work should not be wasted, and that all creatures should not perish for want of another to serve, he filled the earth with humans, sprung from the seed of these two, and placed them over it.

The people were aware of the dangers, but because of the original sin, inherited from their first parents, they began to hate one another. They divided the world between them. And so man, whom God had made perfect and without guile, became embroiled in arguments.

Therefore, because of necessity and divine will, princes were created so that crimes might be controlled. And these same judges, who had the power of life and death, were able, as the agents of the divine will, to decide every man's fortune and standing. The King of Kings requires that monarchs should have the strength to guard Holy Church, the mother of Christianity, from all who would defile her. They must protect her from armed attack, and should maintain peace and justice, which fold each other in their arms like sisters. And so we, who have been raised beyond the dreams of mankind to be Roman Emperor and the right hand of the Almighty, wish to render unto God a double payment for the talent granted us, out of devotion to Jesus Christ, who has given us all that we possess.

Therefore, we will sacrifice a young calf in honor of justice and law-making, first of all providing for that realm which stands in the most need of justice. Therefore, since our kingdom of Sicily has, until now, suffered disorders on account of our youth and our absence, we have decided to provide it with peace and justice, especially as it has always been loyal, resisting enemies both from within and without. It is therefore our wish that only laws approved by us shall be in force in our kingdom of Sicily. We decree that these constitutions shall be observed and that all laws and customs that contradict them shall be abolished. We have ordered that the laws of our predecessors the kings of Sicily shall be included in this code, so that, as far as these our constitutions are concerned, there may be some power and authority both within and without the courts of law. [*Constitutions of Melfi*]

This is an account of the coronation of Richard II of England in 1377:

33. A corporal oath was taken by the archbishop from the king,

1. About conceding and preserving, with the confirmation of his oath, the laws and customs, conceded by ancient, just and devout kings of England, predecessors of the present king, to the people of England, and especially the laws, customs and liberties conceded by the most glorious and holy King Edward to the clergy and people of the aforesaid kingdom.

2. And about serving God, and keeping peace and concord for the Holy Church of God, and for the clergy and people, according to his strength.

3. And about causing to be done, in all his judgments, equal and right justice and decisions in mercy and truth.

4. And also about holding and maintaining the just laws and customs of the church, and about enforcing what the people shall justly and reasonably have chosen and which the king shall protect and strengthen for the honor of God, according to his strength.

The aforesaid archbishop, advancing to the four corners of the platform, expounded and narrated to the whole people how the lord king had taken the oath, inquiring from the same people if they wished to have and obey him as king and liege lord, and they unanimously gave their consent.

When these things had been done, the archbishop began with a loud voice the hymn *Veni Creator Spiritus;* and when this was finished and the archbishop had said certain devout prayers, and a solemn litany had been sung by the prelates and clergy, the aforesaid lord king, whose clothes had been suitably cut open, was anointed with holy oil and chrism on

various parts of his body, according to custom, by the hands
of the aforesaid archbishop on the step of his chair, and at
once he was crowned.

And when the king had been adorned with the sword which
is called Curtana, the scepter, ring, spurs and other regalia, as
was fitting, the magnates and lords standing round him raised
him into his royal chair. [*Close Roll,* Richard II, 1377]

One purpose of this elaborate ritual was to emphasize that the
king derived his authority from God, which meant he could require
obedience from all his subjects. However, the king bound himself by
oath to maintain the laws and customs of the land and to give "equal
and right justice and decisions." There is no mention of law-making,
a concept that was unknown. The king's duty was, through his judges,
to administer and interpret the law, but no more. In practice, the law
was indeed changed during the process of interpreting it and as Parliament and the other courts devised "new remedies for new wrongs,"
but there was no conscious attempt at legislation, as we understand
it. The law derived from God, from nature and from custom, so theo-
retically at least, it was immutable. From this it followed not only
that the king was unable to make law, but also that he was himself
bound by it. He was *"sub Deo et sub lege,"* under God and under the
law. If he went against either, he was a tyrant and, as such, was without authority. Some held that a tyrant should be overthrown, though
others believed that he should be left to God.

THE ADMINISTRATION OF JUSTICE

Upholding peace and justice was not a vague ideal. It was a practical
problem which required practical solutions. The kings of England,
for example, not only established central courts, but sent their judges
to enforce the law throughout the realm. These traveling judges were
known as "justices in eyre," "eyre" meaning "journey." At first, the
system was rather haphazard, but became better organized, especially in the reign of Henry II (1154-1189). Circuits were planned and
judges toured them regularly.

The following are extracts from the *Assize of Clarendon* of 1166 in which the king stated the procedures which the justices in eyre and the sheriffs should follow:

34. In the first place, King Henry, having taken the advice of his barons, in order to preserve peace and maintain justice, has ordered that there shall be an inquiry throughout all the counties and all the hundreds. It shall be made of twelve trustworthy men of each hundred and four trustworthy men of each village, who will swear to tell truthfully whether there be in their hundred or vill any man who is accused or suspected of being a robber, a murderer or a thief, or who is sheltering robbers, murderers or thieves. And the justices must investigate this among themselves, and the sheriffs among themselves.

If any man is accused, on the aforesaid oath, of having been a robber, a murderer or a thief, or having sheltered one, let him be put to the ordeal by water, and let him take an oath that he has not been a robber, a murderer or a thief, or the accomplice of one, to the amount of five shillings, as far as he is aware.

And let the sheriffs who have arrested the accused bring them before the justices without waiting to be summoned. And when robbers or murderers or thieves, or those who shelter them are delivered to the sheriff, let him imprison them without delay.

And in the counties where there are no gaols, let some be made in a town or castle at the king's expense and with timber from one of his woods, so that the sheriffs' officials may be able to guard the accused.

Let no one dwelling within or without a city, borough or castle forbid the sheriffs to enter their land to arrest those accused of being robbers, murderers or thieves, or their accomplices, or outlaws, or those charged with breaking the forest laws. But the king orders that they shall help the sheriffs capture them.

And if a sheriff shall inform another sheriff that men have fled from his county into another, being accused of robbery, or murder, or theft, or of sheltering such men, or breach of the forest laws, let him arrest them. And even if he discovers for himself that such men have fled into his county, let him arrest them and keep them safe, until he has received pledges for them. [*Assize of Clarendon*]

The jury of presentment was not an innovation, but it was the *Assize of Clarendon* which formulated it clearly for the first time.

A SAINTLY KING

Kings were exposed to more temptations than ordinary mortals, but some managed to live good lives. The following is a description of Louis IX of France (1226-1270), written by Jean, lord of Joinville, who was one of his courtiers:

35. Louis IX so scorned the vanities of this world that he would never wear ermine, squirrel fur or scarlet cloth, and his stirrups and spurs were not gilded. His clothes were of gray woolen cloth, trimmed with fur of deer, hares and lambs.

Louis had no liking for fine food. He never had anything cooked specially for him, but ate whatever was placed before him. To drink, he had water mixed with wine, varying the amount of the water according to the strength of the wine. He always made sure the poor were fed, and when they had eaten he gave them money.

When minstrels played to entertain him after dinner, he always allowed them to finish their music before grace was said. Then he would stand, and the priests would say grace.

Sometimes when we called on him, he would sit at the foot of his bed. If a friar offered to read him a book he would say, "Don't read to me. The best book after meals is friendly conversation, when everyone says exactly what he likes." When important guests came to dine with the king, they always found him excellent company.

Louis greatly loved his people, as is shown by what he said to his eldest son when lying near to death at Fontainbleau. "My dear son, I entreat you to make sure your people love you. I would sooner a Scot came from Scotland to rule this kingdom justly, rather than that you should govern it badly, and for all to see." [The Scots were considered barbarians.]

The king was always careful of what he said. Never did I hear him speak ill of anyone, and neither did he utter the name of the devil, even though this is commonly done and is displeasing to God.

Once, Louis asked me if I washed the feet of the poor on Maundy Thursday. "Your Majesty," I replied, "that is a terrible notion! I would never wash the feet of such dreadful people."

"That," he replied, "is a wicked thing to say. You should never be too proud to follow Our Lord's example. For love of Him and for love of me, you should wash the feet of the poor."

After hearing Mass on a summer's day, Louis often went to the wood of Vincennes, near Paris, where he would sit, leaning against an oak, and we would all gather round him. Those who had anything to ask of him, could do so, without the interference of any official. In summer, I have seen him administer justice in the public gardens of Paris. He dressed modestly in a plain, woolen tunic, a black cape and a hat of white peacock's feathers. A carpet would be laid on the ground, where we could sit, and those who had cases for him to consider stood nearby. Then he would pass judgment on each case, just as he did in the wood of Vincennes. [*Life of St. Louis*]

Jean de Joinville was the king's friend, so this eulogy should be treated with some caution, but others must have held similar views, for Louis was canonized in 1297.

CHAPTER 5
THE ROYAL COURT

THE CAROLINGIAN COURT

In A.D. 882, Hincmar, bishop of Rheims, wrote a treatise for the benefit of the young Carloman, king of the Franks. In it he described how the royal court had been organized under Charlemagne (768-814):

36. The chaplain had under his control the supervision of the clergy of the palace. Associated with him was the archchancellor. Under him were wise, intelligent and faithful men, who were to record the imperial demands without demanding excessive payment, and who would faithfully keep the royal secrets. Under these officers, the sacred palace was administered through these officials: the chamberlain, the count of the palace, the seneschal, the wine steward, the constable, the master of lodgings, four chief hunters and one falconer. Under them were other officials, such as the porter, keeper of the purse, dispenser, and keeper of the utensils. These, too, had subordinates, such as wardens of the forest, keepers of the kennels, hunters of beavers, and others. [De ordine palatii]

Elsewhere, Hincmar says that the count of the palace was the equal of the chaplain. The one managed secular affairs, and the other spiritual. Hincmar describes their duties:

37. The chaplain had the supervision over everything which concerned the Church. He settled disputes and considered ecclesiastical questions of every kind that reached the palace. He saw to it that the only issues which were brought before the king were those which could not be settled

without him. Further, he was responsible for everything within the palace that concerned the Church. Whoever in the entire palace sought spiritual consolation or advice, found it without fail in him. If he saw that anyone who did not ask his help still had need of it, he strove to rescue him from his wicked thoughts and works and to turn him to the way of salvation.

The count of the palace, among many other duties, was responsible for the just settlement of all disputes which were brought to the palace. He also reversed bad judgments. By this he earned favor with God by reason of his justice, and among men for his observance of the laws. If there was a case which the secular laws did not cover, or for which pagan customs decreed a crueler punishment than Christianity allowed, the matter was brought to the king. Then, in consultation with experts in both sacred and secular law, the king would make a decision which would, if possible, respect both laws. If this was not possible, the secular law would be ignored and the law of God followed. [Ibid.]

These were the duties of other officials:

38. To three officers, the seneschal, the wine steward and the constable, fell this responsibility. They were to inform all local officials, as soon as possible, about the times, places and seasons of the king's arrival and the duration of his stay, so that they could collect and prepare what was needed. Otherwise, if the local officials learned of this too late and performed their duties at the wrong time, or in undue haste, then the royal party might suffer serious inconvenience. Mainly, this was the duty of the wine steward and the constable, but the seneschal was concerned as well, since he was responsible for water and fodder for the horses.

Similarly, the four hunters and the fifth falconer had to carry out their own duties. They had to decide how many hunters were to be kept at the palace at various times. They also assigned men to designated places for the purpose of carrying on the hunt. In these offices, it is difficult to calculate the correct number of men or of dogs or of falcons. Therefore it was for them to decide how many and of what sort these men and animals might be. [Ibid.]

THE COURT OF HENRY II OF ENGLAND, 1154-1189

As the last document suggests, the royal court was frequently on the move. Communications were so bad that it was often easier to take the court to the provisions than the provisions to the court. Consequently the court traveled the country like a swarm of locusts, devouring as it went. In England, there were numerous royal manors, scattered all over the realm. Instead of knight service, each had the duty of supporting the court for a day or two in the year. Peter of Blois, a distinguished scholar of the twelfth century, was invited to England by Henry II. He says what it was like to travel with the king:

39. I marvel how any man can suffer the miseries of court life, who has long been used to learning and universities. For courtiers know neither order nor reason nor measure in their meals, or in their ridings abroad, or in their nightly watchings.

Court chaplains and knights are served with bread hastily made, without leaven, from the dregs of the ale tub, leaden bread, bread of tares, bread unbaken. The wine is turned sour or moldy; thick, greasy, stale, flat and tasting of pitch from the cask. I have sometimes seen even great lords served with wine so muddy that a man must needs close his eyes and clench his teeth, wry-mouthed and shuddering, and filtering the stuff rather than drinking. The ale which men drink in that place is horrid to the taste and abominable to the sight. Also sick and whole beasts are sold at random, with fishes even four days old; yet shall not all this corruption and stench reduce the price by one penny; for the servants care not whether an unhappy guest fall sick or die, as long as their lords' tables are served with a multitude of dishes. We who sit at meat must needs fill our bellies with carrion and become graves, as it were, for corpses. If the court dwell longer than usual in any town, some courtiers are left behind to die.

I cannot endure the vexations of the royal stewards – fawning flatterers, wicked backbiters, unprincipled extortioners; wearisome with their importunities for gifts, ungrateful for benefits received, malignant to all such as are unwilling to give again and again. I have known many who have given generously to such stewards; yet, when with much labor they had sought their lodging after a long day's journey, while their supper was yet half-cooked, or again while they sat at meat – nay, even while they slept on their bed, these stewards would come swelling with pride and contumely, cut the horses' halters, cast forth the baggage recklessly, and perhaps with grievous loss, and expel the guests with so little ceremony that these (for all their wealth and their provision of traveling bed-gear) had nowhere to lay their heads that night.

This again adds to the courtiers' misery, that if the king has promised to stay anywhere, and especially if the herald has proclaimed this as the royal will, then be sure that he will set out at daybreak, mocking all men's expectation by his sudden change of purpose. Whereby it often happens

that such courtiers as have let themselves be bled, or have taken some purgative, must yet follow their prince forthwith without regard to their own bodies, and, putting their lives at risk, hasten blindfold to ruin for dread of losing that which they have not, nor never shall have. Then may ye see men rush forth like madmen, sumpter-mules jostling sumpter-mules and chariots clashing against chariots in frantic confusion, a very Pandemonium made visible.

Or again, if the king has proclaimed his purpose of setting out for a certain place with the morrow's dawn, then will he surely change his purpose; doubt not but that he will lie abed till mid-day. Here wait the sumpters, standing under their loads, the chariots idly silent, the outriders asleep, the royal merchants in anxious expectation, and all murmuring together. Men flock round the court prostitutes and vintners, a kind of courtiers who often know the palace secrets, to get tidings of the king's journey. For the king's train swarms with play actors and washerwomen, dicers and flatterers, taverners, wagerers, buffoons, barbers, tumblers, and all birds of that feather.

Often, have I seen how, when the king slept and all things were in quiet silence, there leapt down a word from the royal quarters, naming that city or town for which the court must now set out. After the long weariness of delay and suspense, we solaced ourselves with the expectation of sleeping there, where, as we hoped, lodging and food would abundantly be found; for so great was the press, so confused and tumultuous the wandering crowds of horse and foot, that the abyss seemed to have been opened, and hell to vomit forth his legions. Yet, when our outriders had gone the whole day's journey, then again would the king change his purpose and lodge elsewhere, having perhaps a single house and victuals enough for himself alone, whereof no other might share: yea, and I verily believe that he has found in our misery, a keener zest for his own pleasures.

We therefore, wandering for three or four miles through unknown forests, and often in the black darkness, thought ourselves fortunate if we came upon some vile and sordid hovel. Often, the courtiers would fight bitterly for mere huts and contend with drawn swords for a lair which would have been unworthy of contention among swine. How we and our beasts fared meanwhile on such a night may well be imagined. I myself was so divided from my train that it was scarce possible to collect the scattered remnants within three days. [*Letter to the Royal Chaplains of Henry II*]

THE LATE MIDDLE AGES

Down to the thirteenth century, the English court consisted of knights and nobles, the officers of the household and the great officers of state with their staffs of clerics. All were men, and nearly all their functions were practical. From the fourteenth century, though, courts were centers of culture and many women attended them. Court poets became popular, the most famous of these in England being Geoffrey Chaucer (c. 1340-1400). Poets read lengthy works, usually romantic tales of various kinds, to audiences of courtiers. They read slowly, and in installments, so their performances were the equivalent of modern soap operas. The Flemish chronicler and poet Jean Froissart read his *Melidor* at the court of the count of Foix during the winter of 1388-1389. It took him ten weeks, and as the epic contains 31,000 lines, he probably read about 500 a night. Froissart said, "Every night after supper I read to the count, and while I read, there was none durst speak any word, because he would that I should be well understood." The count, though, was a trying patron, since he refused to keep the normal meal times of ten in the morning for dinner and five in the afternoon for supper. "His usage was always that it was high noon or he arose out of his bed, and supped ever at midnight." The readings took place after supper.

Royal courts of the late Middle Ages were magnificent. The following account of the court of Edward IV of England was

54

written by a companion of the German envoy of the king of
Bohemia in 1466:

> 40. The king soon allowed my lord to appear before him.
> Then we saw the tremendously great reverence which his
> servants showed towards him, and how mighty earls had to
> kneel before him. But he gave my lord and his companions
> his hand, and my lord then told him about his journey and
> the reasons for it. The king took great delight in this and
> was very friendly to my lord. The king is a very handsome,
> upright man and has the most splendid court that one can
> find in all Christendom. After this, nine days later, he enter-
> tained my lord Leon and all his noble companions and gave
> him a very splendid meal, of over fifty dishes, according to
> their custom.
>
> On another day, the king summoned us to his court, on the
> morning when the queen left her childbed to go to church with a
> splendid procession, accompanied by many priests and many
> school-boys singing and carrying lights. There followed a great
> band of matrons and maidens from the country and from Lon-
> don, too, who had been invited to attend. Then came a great num-
> ber of trumpeters, pipers and drummers. Then followed the king's
> choristers, about 42 of them, who sang excellently. Then marched

> 24 heralds and pur-
> suivants, followed by
> about 60 earls and
> knights. After them
> came the queen, es-
> corted by two dukes,
> with a canopy carried
> over her. Behind her
> walked her mother,
> with about 60 maid-
> ens and ladies. So she
> heard a sung office
> and then she left the
> church with the

same procession as before and returned to her palace. Then all who had taken part in the procession stayed to the banquet. They seated themselves, men and women, clerical and lay, each according to his rank, and they filled four large halls.

My lord and his companions and the noblest lords were specially served in the hall and at the tables where the king and his court are accustomed to dine. They entertained my lord so splendidly that you would not believe how lavish was the feast.

While we were eating, the king's gifts were distributed to all the trumpeters, pipers, jesters, and heralds, the heralds alone receiving 400 nobles. Every man to whom a reward had been given went about the tables, and called aloud the sum which the king had given him. [Gabriel Tetzel, *The Travels of Leon von Rozmital*]

When the visitors had finished eating, they were taken to a "particularly splendid and decorated hall," where the queen was now to have her meal:

41. My lord and his companions were seated in a corner, so that they might witness the great splendor of the arrangements. The queen sat alone at table in a costly golden chair. The queen's mother and the

king's sister had to stand below. And if the queen talked with them, they had to kneel before her until she drank water. Not until the first dish was set before her were they allowed to sit down. The ladies and maidens and all who served dishes to the queen, even if they were powerful earls, had nevertheless to kneel, as long as she was eating. The feast lasted for three hours, and many costly dishes were served to the queen, and her mother, and the king's sister and others; of these dishes it would take too long to write. All were silent; not a word was spoken.

After the banquet, the dancing began. The queen remained seated in her chair. Her mother knelt before her, standing up only at intervals. The king's sister danced with two dukes in stately dances, and made impressive courtesies to the queen such as I have never seen elsewhere; nor have I witnessed such outstandingly beautiful maidens. Among these young ladies were eight duchesses and about thirty countesses, and the others were all daughters of men of high lineage. After the dancing, the king's choristers entered and sang. [Ibid.]

The queen was, formerly, Elizabeth Woodville. As a young widow, she had resisted the king's attempts to seduce her, leaving him with no option but to marry her. This was quite remarkable, for both parties to a royal marriage were almost always of royal rank and the union was made for important reasons of state. Elizabeth's father was a knight and her mother a dowager duchess, so, although of gentle birth, she was not sprung from the highest in the land, and it must have galled the old nobility that they had to pay her so much deference.

CHAPTER 6
FEUDALISM IN SPAIN

FOR HUNDREDS OF YEARS, the Iberian Peninsula was part of the Roman Empire, but in A.D. 414 it fell to the Visigoths. They established themselves as a ruling aristocracy, while the Hispano-Romans continued to live in much the same way as they always had done. This was similar to what happened in much of the western Empire, but thereafter the history of Iberia was somewhat different. One reason was the Pyrenees, which separate it from the rest of Europe, but even more important was its conquest by Muslim invaders from North Africa. They are known collectively as "Moors," though they were, in fact diverse, many of the rank and file being Berbers while their leaders were Arabs.

The Moors first crossed the Straits of Gibraltar in A.D. 711 and, within a few years, they had overrun most of Iberia. They then swept over the Pyrenees and were not checked until Charles Martel defeated them at Poitiers in A.D. 732. They then withdrew to Iberia. Here, a string of Christian states made its appearance along the northern extremity, including León, Castile, Navarre, Aragon, Catalonia and, later, Portugal. These states gradually won back territory from the Moors, the lion's share going to the united kingdoms of Castile and León. This *"reconquista"* was slow, because the Christians often fought each other and, when they did so, they sought allies among the Moors. These, too, were frequently at each others' throats, so that there was a constantly shifting quicksand of rival coalitions, Christians and Moors fighting against Christians and Moors. Spain's great national hero, El Cid, was not the man portrayed by Charlton Heston, but a hard-headed mercenary who fought for whatever ruler offered him the most, regardless of race or religion. However, by the end of the thirteenth century, the only Moorish kingdom remaining was Granada in the deep south. This survived until 1492.

There was a further problem. Much of the territory between the Christian and Moorish states was a deserted no-man's land, so that when the Christians did establish control over any of it, they had to people it, if they were to have any hope of keeping it.

The documents in this chapter are of interest because they show the differences caused by the special problems of Iberia, though there were, at the same time, many similarities with the rest of Europe.

Here, first of all, is a description of a rebellion of A.D. 654 which shows the conditions that favored the growth of feudalism, namely, chronic disorder and the yearning which people had for a powerful protector:

42. In that time a pestiferous, crazy man, Froja, rebelled, along with evil accomplices to his crime. He deceived that orthodox, devout worshipper of God, Prince Recesvinto, and, bursting with pride, invaded Christian lands. Encouraged by this crime, the proud race of the Basques came down from the Pyrenees and marched on the land of Iberia, depopulating and devastating it. They spilt the blood of many innocent Christians. Some were mortally wounded by the sword, others by lances, and the majority by various weapons thrown at them; a great many captives were carried off by force, an immense booty was seized. This sacrilegious war was carried into the churches, destroying the sacred altars. Most of the clergy had their throats slit, and the corpses were so numerous that they could not be buried and were left to the birds and the dogs. For this reason we shut ourselves in the city of Zaragosa, recently fortified, and waited for the arrival of the prince, which had been promised; we implored with the most fervent prayers the pity of Almighty God, begging that he would not allow the rebel yoke to be fastened on our necks, and that he would lend the strength of his right arm to our most pious prince against a most impious enemy. But the Lord at once heard the pleadings of

his unfortunate people and the supplication of our most merciful prince. A powerful soldier sent from heaven supported him with his omnipotence and condemned the rebel to sudden death. He gave the one the copious palm of victory and hurled down on the other the ignominy of an atrocious death. [*Epistola ad Quiricum Barcinonensem, Tajón*]

The following, a document of the thirteenth century, gives a Spanish account of "those who fight," whom it terms "defenders":

43. Defenders are one of the three orders that God ordained should sustain the world. Those who plead with God on behalf of the people are called *oradores* [people who pray]; those who toil on the land and produce the things that allow men to live and keep themselves are called "workers"; and those whose duty is defense are called "defenders." Therefore the ancients put much store by the careful choice of such men, because they needed three qualities, force, honor and power. We have shown what the people should do with waste land, producing offspring to inhabit it, and working it to enjoy its fruits, and discovering what riches it may contain, and defending it and extending it at the expense of enemies, which should be the concern of everyone. But this last is, above all, the duty of the knights, whom the ancients styled "defenders," partly because they are the most honorable, and partly because they were instituted especially to defend the land and extend it. [*Partida 2a, titulo xxi*]

The following comes from a code of customs that governed feudal relationships in Aragon in the early twelfth century:

44. If anyone denies his lord the possession of his castle, when he ought to yield it, and then disobeys the order, if the lord can seize the castle, it will be lawful for him to hold it, along with its dependent fiefs, until the offender has recompensed the lord for all his expenses and losses in taking the castle and guarding it, and has undertaken, swearing with the holy scriptures in his hands, that he will never again deny the lord possession.

If any from the rank of viscount to lesser knight should die intestate and without any obvious heir, it shall be lawful for the lord to give the fief to any of the children of the deceased that they may choose.

The castellans of castles which they hold for their lords may not appoint any subordinate castellans without the consent of their lords But if they do so, and the lords know it and do not object, then those appointed may remain. But if the lords do know and object, then they must leave.

If anyone alienates his fief to another without the agreement of his lord, if the lord knows and objects, he can hold the fief for as long as he likes; but if he knows and does not object, he may not hold the fief, but may require the service of it from the donor or the recipient, whichever he prefers. If the service is refused, it will be lawful for him to hold the fief and keep it in demesne until he is compensated twofold for the lost service, and is solemnly promised that it will never again be withheld.

Whosoever ought to obey the summons to the lord's hosts and cavalcades and fails to do so, let him compensate the lord twofold, if the lord wishes, or pay compensation for all the expenses and losses incurred by the lord as the result of his default. Similarly, if any of the knights lose anything in hosts, campaigns and services of their lords, then let the lords compensate them, provided they can prove their claims by oath.

If a lord requires extra services from his man, let him increase his benefice. If he fails in this, let the man do as he was accustomed to do, and perform the services to which he was accustomed.

Whoever deserts his lord during a war, or who, with evil intent, separates himself from him during battle, must lose all he holds from his lord.

Whoever breaks faith with his lord, or abandons his fief, let the lord occupy all the vassal holds from him, and keep it until he returns to his homage and acknowledges his lord's rights and makes amends under oath for the wrong which he did, whereupon he may reoccupy his fief.

Whosoever despises his lord or, out of pride, breaks faith with him, must lose for ever all that he holds from him and return any of the lord's possessions that he might have, and leave his service.

Whosoever deliberately kills his lord or his legitimate heir, or commits adultery with his wife, or abandons his castle, or does him any harm which he cannot put right, he must remain at the will of the lord and do whatever is required of him.

Similarly, if the lord treats his knight unjustly, or dishonors him, the crown must defend him and keep him in its care.

Any wrong which a man may do to his lord, or the lord to his man, without denial of right or breach of faith, must be resolved by both parties.

All men, from viscounts to lesser knights, must swear on the holy scriptures that they will be faithful to the crown and to its honor; that is to say, those whom the crown may require to do so. [*Usatici Barchinone*]

The bishop of Barcelona grants the castle of Alba to Guitardo de Muradén, A.D. 978:

45. This is an agreement which Bishop Vivas makes, in the company of many of his clergy, with Don Guitardo de Muradén. Be it known to all men that I, Bishop Vivas, with the counsel of the clergy of the church of St. Cross and St. Eulalia, and with the consent of the most pious marquis, our prince, Count Borrello, make an agreement between us and the aforesaid Guitardo concerning the castle of Alba, with all its territory, both what is built and what is to be built, so that you may hold and possess it on our behalf and may give to me and my successors the right to use the same castle of Alba as often as we may ask, without any obstructive opposition.

And you give me surety under oath to me and my successors, and you will not appoint castellans without my consent, and they must always pay me homage and keep faith with me. And in the territories of the said castle I keep for myself the churches with their tithes and offerings and my lands that lie between the castle of Alba and the castle of Ceume and my demesne known as the Holy Crosses above the banks of the River Gaiá, with all their boundaries and with all their dependencies, with their mills and water courses and springs, and all that men may use, without you, Guitardo having any seigneurial rights, or the castellans of the aforesaid castle of Alba. And what remains of the lands of the aforesaid castle you may possess, rendering faithful service to me and my successors.

And I, Guitardo, agree with you, Bishop Vivas, my lord, and with your successors, that I will keep faith with you in what concerns your person and the aforementioned castle, and will give you and your successors the right to use the castle, willingly and peacefully, as often as you may ask, for yourself or those whom you may send, and I will do service of "host and cavalcade" and other services such as a vassal should perform for his lord. [*Cartas de población y franquicia de Cataluña*]

The rulers of Catalonia of the eleventh century make a grant of uninhabited land to some vassals. They are so anxious that it should be peopled that half of it is an allod, that is, an outright gift rather than a fief, for which services would be due:

46. In the name of Christ, I Ermesenda, countess by the grace of God, with my son Berenguer, marquis and count, and with his wife Sancha, by virtue of our munificence, generously make a grant to you, Guinedilda and [several other names follow]; and we give you our uninhabited lands situated in the proximity of the frontier of the county of Ausona, with the mountain and the castle which is called Cervera, which you constructed as a defense against attack by the

pagans, before any other frontier settlers arrived, and the tower, already built which you have in your charge, together with all the hills that lie in its boundaries.

All these lands belong to us by virtue of the generosity of our predecessors Borrell and Raimundo, counts and marquesses of blessed memory and also by the royal authority which we exercise over these lands, as did our ancestors. [The boundaries of the castle's dependencies follow.]

All those things that are within the aforementioned boundaries we give to you the aforementioned men and aforementioned women, with this condition, that, in so far as God will permit, you will reclaim the waste lands, cultivating them and building habitations for men, along with castles and towers. And that neither you nor your heirs and successors will alienate the aforementioned lands to any other lord, save to us and our heirs.

Let half of the aforementioned lands which are within the aforementioned boundaries be your allod, and yours to do with as you wish, both yourselves and your heirs and successors. The other half you will occupy as the vassals of us and of our heirs and you and your successors will hold it securely by the good faith of ourselves and of our heirs. [Ibid.]

In 1173 Alfonso VII of León adopted the grandiose title of "emperor." His coronation included some celebrations that would have been considered unusual in other parts of Europe:

47. In the year 1173, the king chose 4 June, the Feast of the Pentecost, as the date for the celebration in the royal city of León, and summoned the archbishops, bishops, counts, princes, dukes and judges of all his realms. On the day appointed, the king arrived, accompanied by his wife, Doña Berenguela, by her sister the Princess Doña Sancha, and by García, king of Pamplona. Also there gathered a great crowd of monks and clergy, as well as large numbers of ordinary people, who came to see, hear or recite the divine offices.

On the first day of the ceremony, all the hierarchies, greater and less, met with the king in St. Mary's Church and did those things which Our Lord Jesus Christ inspired them to do, as well as others appropriate for the salvation of the souls of the faithful. On the second day, Pentecost, the archbishops, bishops, abbots, nobles, gentry and all the people met for the second time in St. Mary's Church and, along with King García and the king's sister, in accordance with divine will, they proclaimed Alfonso emperor. By virtue of this, King García and King Zafadola of the Moors and Count Raymond of Barcelona and Count Alfonso of Toledo and many counts and dukes of Gascony and France, should pay him absolute obedience.

With the king wearing a most magnificent cloak, embroidered with great beauty, they placed on his temples a crown of pure gold, encrusted with precious stones, and when they had placed the scepter in his hands, King García supporting him by the right arm, and the bishop of León by the left, they took him before the altar of St. Mary in the center of a retinue of bishops and abbots, singing the *Te Deum Laudamus* and proclaiming, "Long live Emperor Alfonso." And when he had been blessed, they celebrated a solemn mass. And then everyone went back to his lodgings. But the king ordered a grand banquet in the royal palace, for the counts, princes and dukes. He also ordered that the bishops, abbots and the rest should be handsomely rewarded, and at the same time he ordered the distribution of generous alms of wheat and clothing to the poor.

On the third day, the emperor and everyone else met in the royal palace and dealt with those matters that concerned the liberation of the whole of Spain; and the emperor issued decrees and laws for all his kingdom as had been done in the days of his grandfather, King Alfonso.

And he ordered the reestablishment of all the inhabitants and families in their former churches, from which they had been excluded illegally or unjustly; and he ordered that the towns and lands that had been destroyed during the war should be peopled and that vines and all manner of trees should be planted and he ordered the judges to root out the crimes of those who were taken acting unjustly or against the laws of the powers or judges. These last passed sentence with impartial justice, condemning some to be hung and others to the loss of their feet or arms, showing no more indulgence to the rich than the poor, but punishing according to the gravity of the crime. Moreover the emperor commanded that there should be no indulgence shown to the wicked, just as God commanded Moses, "Do not tolerate evil men." Some of these perpetrators of wickedness were arrested in his very presence and hung from the gallows.

He also ordered the mayors of Toledo and the inhabitants of the border lands to muster armies from time to time and make war every year on the infidel Moors, and not to be intimidated by their cities or fortresses, but to redeem everything for God and the Christian law.

When all these measures had been taken, and the meeting ended, each one went his way, singing with jubilation and praising the emperor with these words, "Blessed be you and blessed be the kingdom of your forefathers and blessed be the Almighty who made heaven and earth, the sea and all therein, for you have come to us and granted us the blessing which you had promised us for keeping faith." [*Crónica Aldefonsi Imperatoris*]

The following is part of an address to the crown made by the Cortés, or parliament, of León and Castile in 1445:

48. Most high and mighty prince and most illustrious king and lord, your humble servants, the representatives of the cities and towns, kiss your hands and feet with devout reverence and most humbly place themselves at your great mercy, fully aware of the misdeeds of the people. In recent times, God has permitted sundry tumults and rebellions and scandals in your kingdom, in the course of which numbers

67

of your subjects have died, forgetting the natural law under which even the bees have a prince and the ants follow a leader whom they respect and obey. The same is true of divine law, which expressly forbids anyone to dare to touch his king or prince, this being an affront to God, or should even show any desire that the king should suffer ill, or even think about it, for he should be considered the vicar of God and honored for his majesty and that none should dare resist him, for those who resist their king are seen as resisting the ordinances of God, so that all should fulfill their obligations and duties, not only fearing the wrath of God and the ill and the pain which they may suffer from it, but also to keep their consciences clear. [End of period. The Spanish sentence is 119 words long.] And those who do the contrary and do not obey their princes and kings are for that reason guilty and deserving of death. [*Cortés de los antiguos reinos de León et Castille*]

As in other countries, theory and practice did not always agree. The following is an account of the "Farce of Avila" of 1465:

49. When the king arrived at Salamanca, the archbishop of Toledo seized the city of Avila, and when that had been done there came thither those nobles who were in Plasencia with Prince Don Alonso. The following assembled, [a list of names follows] with other nobles and knights of lower rank. They ordered that a scaffold should be erected outside the town on a large piece of level ground, and on the scaffold they placed an effigy of the king seated on a chair, and dressed in mourning. He had a crown on his head, and held a sword in front of him and a mace in his hand. When this was ready, all the aforementioned came to the scaffold, accompanied by Prince Don Alonso. The greater nobles and the prince occupied much of the space on the scaffold, and the remainder took their places around the effigy. From there, in loud voices, they ordered that a proclamation should be read, which contained more of vanity than matters of

substance, and which accused the king of four evils. In the first place that he deserved to lose the royal dignity; and then Don Alonso Carillo, archbishop of Toledo, approached and took the crown from his head. Secondly that he deserved to lose the administration of justice; then Don Alvaro de Zuñiga, count of Plasencia, approached and took away the sword that he held in front of him. Thirdly, that he deserved to lose the government of the kingdom; and Don Rodrigo Pimental, count of Benevente, approached and took away the mace which he held in his hand. Fourthly, that he deserved to lose the throne and title of king; and Don Diego Lopez de Zuñiga approached and knocked the effigy from its chair, saying wild and seditious words. [A lengthy diatribe against the perpetrators follows.] Then, when the downfall of the effigy was complete, these good servants of the king, in their gratitude for the favors they had received from his majesty [Spanish irony], raised Don Alonso above the scaffold. Lifting him on to their shoulders, they and the nobles cried in loud voices, "Castile for King Don Alonso." This said, the trumpets and drums rang out with resounding clangor. [*Crónica del rey don Enrique Cuarto*]

CHAPTER 7
RICHARD II OF ENGLAND
1377-1399

THERE WERE CRISES of kingship at different times and in different countries during the Middle Ages, but the reign of Richard II makes a particularly interesting case study.

Richard was born in 1367. He was the son of Edward the Black Prince, one of England's most famous soldiers, and heir to King Edward III. The Black Prince, though, died in 1376, a year before his father, so Richard inherited the throne from his grandfather in 1377.

The new king was only ten years old when he was crowned with all the ceremony described in Chapter 4 [reading 33]. The boy would have understood little of the oath that he took, but he found himself the center of an elaborate, magnificent ritual, and, being impressionable, must have gained a tremendous sense of his own importance. In 1381, when Richard was fourteen, there occurred the famous Peasants' Revolt, during which London was captured. At the height of the troubles, while everyone on the royal side wavered, the king rode alone into the heart of the rebel army, and persuaded the men to end their revolt. This bravery won him praise and increased the high opinion he already had of himself. It also confirmed his gambling instincts, persuading him that he could play for high stakes and win.

These accounts, written by a monk of Westminster Abbey, throw further light on the king's character: *Leo̧* 1386

> 50. On the feast of the Purification of the Virgin, the king held court at Windsor. With him was the king of Armenia, whom, smiling with pleasure, he strove to honor in every way. He gave him a piece of silver plate, shaped like a ship,

to be used as an alms dish. It was three feet long and very valuable. This, he filled to the brim with gold. The visitor accepted this and other gifts before his departure, but near Calais, he lost most of them to thieves. [*Westminster Chronicle*, 1386]

51. During this period the king at his own expense married some of the queen's countrywomen to men of rank; in his early years, our king was so generous that when anyone made a request of him, he granted it immediately. Sometimes, he even anticipated the wishes of the suppliants and often granted more than they asked. So lavish was he that the Crown's property and the revenues of the royal exchequer were nearly all granted piecemeal to different people who made demands for one thing or another. Having squandered his substance in this way, he was compelled to oppress the common folk with taxes, so that the poor complain bitterly and say that they can no longer sustain the burden. [Ibid.]

CHAPTER 7. RICHARD II OF ENGLAND

[Note Richard married Anne of Bohemia in 1382, when they were both aged fifteen. The generous treatment of the queen's followers caused resentment among the English nobility.]

The archbishop of Canterbury provoked the following incident by lecturing the king on the behavior of his advisers:

> 52. On the same day, the king dined with the mayor of London. After the meal, he boarded his barge on the Thames, and between his own palace and that of the archbishop at Lambeth, he met the archbishop who was coming to see him under the safe-conduct of the earl of Buckingham. The archbishop repeated the remarks which he had made in the morning, whereupon the king drew his sword and would have run him through, had not the earl of Buckingham, Sir John Devereux and Sir Thomas Trivet held him back by force. The king was so angry with the three men, that in their fear they leapt from his barge into the archbishop's boat. [Ibid., 1385]

Richard had many good points. There is a long tradition of infidelity in the English royal family, which is still maintained, but Richard was a model husband, quite devoted to his rather plain wife. When she died in 1394, he ordered that the place of her death, Sheen Palace, should be burnt to the ground.

Richard owed much to his uncle, John of Gaunt, who never wavered in his loyalty to the crown. As he was the most powerful of the king's subjects, his support guaranteed Richard's security. Gaunt's main ambition, though, was to become king of Castile and in 1386 he left for Spain. Richard was soon in trouble.

It was a vassal's duty to counsel his lord and as far as the great nobles of England were concerned, this was also a privilege, since it gave them a say in the management of the country. Richard, though, chose to ignore them and governed with the help of his personal friends. Chief among them was Robert de Vere, earl of Oxford. Oxford was the poorest of the English earldoms, but Richard made de Vere marquess of Dublin and duke of Ireland, so promoting him over the heads of men who despised him.

Five of the magnates now conspired against the king. They were Thomas of Woodstock, earl of Gloucester, Richard Fitzalan, earl of Arundel, Thomas Beauchamp, earl of Warwick and two younger men, Henry Bolingbroke, earl of Derby and Thomas Mowbray, earl of Nottingham. Gloucester was one of the king's uncles, while Derby was the eldest son of John of Gaunt. They shrank from a personal attack on Richard, but they accused five of his advisers of taking advantage of his youth and "accroaching the royal power." This offense was high treason. The form of accusation was an "appeal," so the five nobles who made it are known as the "Lords Appellant."

De Vere gathered an army, but it was surrounded at Radcot Bridge on the Thames. He abandoned his men and escaped abroad. In 1388 the five accused were tried by Parliament, sitting as a court of law, and all were found guilty of high treason. Two more had escaped, like de Vere, but Sir Robert Tresilian and Sir Nicholas Brembre suffered the horrible fate of traitors.

It was now the turn of lesser men, including Sir Simon Burley, an honorable and popular member of the royal court. The queen herself went on her knees before Gloucester, pleading for Burley's life, while even Derby and Nottingham would have shown him mercy. The other Appellants, though, were adamant, and only consented to reduce Burley's punishment to beheading. As for Richard, he was shocked into submission.

The Appellants were now, effectively, the rulers of England, but they had no coherent policies and achieved no more than Richard's favorites had done. Their support dwindled while the king regained his composure. This was what happened in 1389:

> 53. In the same year the king, led by the advice of certain whisperers, convoked the magnates and many worthy men of the realm together, and suddenly entered the council house, where they were awaiting him. Seating himself, he asked how old he was. They replied that he was now twenty years old. [He was twenty-two.] "Then," he said, "I am of full age to govern my house and household and also my kingdom. It seems to me unjust that my state should be worse

than that of the least person in the kingdom. Surely any heir of my kingdom when he has reached the age of twenty years and his parent is dead, is permitted to conduct his own affairs freely. Why, therefore, should this be denied to me, when it is conceded by law to anyone else of lower rank?"

The astonished barons replied that nothing ought to be subtracted from his rights, and that he ought to have the rule of his kingdom.

At this, the king exclaimed, "Well! Know that I have for long been ruled by tutors; and it was not possible for me to act without them. Now henceforth I will remove those from my council, and, as heir of lawful age, I will appoint whom I will to my council, and conduct my own affairs. And I order that in the first place the chancellor shall resign to me his seal."

And when the archbishop of York had returned his seal, the king collected it in a fold in his dress and suddenly rose and went out and after a short while he came back and sat down again, and gave the seal to William of Wykeham, bishop of Winchester, although he was very reluctant to take it. And he created nine other officials, most of them former officials, using in all things his own judgment and authority. The duke of Gloucester and the earl of Warwick, and many other worthy persons, he removed from his council and added others who were pleasing in his eyes. [Thomas of Walsingham, *Historia Anglicana*]

Meanwhile, John of Gaunt's attempt to seize the throne of Castile had been a disaster and later in 1389, he returned to England. This ensured some stability, so an uneasy peace followed. Richard pretended he was reconciled to the Appellants, though he was only biding his time.

Having resumed power, Richard followed an enlightened policy towards neighboring countries. In 1394, he took an army to Ireland, but he used a minimum of force, preferring to win over the Irish chiefs by confirming them in possession of their lands and by granting them honors. In 1388, the Scots had won an important battle at Otterburn, and while they had their tails up, it would have been folly to antagonize France. Annual truces were made, followed by one of twenty-eight years in 1396. At the same time, Richard married Isabelle, the eldest daughter of Charles VI. The marriage was by proxy, for the new queen was only seven.

Peace with France was not only sound policy. Richard made it plain that he disapproved of the war, complaining to parliament of the *"tres grandes meschiefs et destructions de Guerre* [war] *entre les deux Roialmes."* The English nobility could not deny the good sense of Richard's attitude, but they resented it, none the less. They viewed France as a happy hunting ground for plunder and ransoms, and sighed for the days when Richard's father and grandfather had led them on profitable expeditions to that country.

At home, Richard strengthened his position, cultivating the knightly class and creating his own private army of retainers. By 1397, he felt strong enough to take revenge on the Appellants. He invited Gloucester, Arundel and Warwick to a banquet. Gloucester pleaded illness, Arundel shut himself in his castle of Reigate and only Warwick obeyed the summons. Richard greeted him cordially, entertained him to a sumptuous banquet, and then arrested him. Arundel was induced to leave his castle when Richard swore an oath that he would not be harmed. He was imprisoned immediately. Richard went in person to arrest Gloucester and, in reply to his plea for mercy, told him he would have just as much mercy as he had shown Simon Burley. He was despatched to the royal castle of Calais, from where the following missive was sent. Gloucester might have composed it voluntarily, he might have done so under duress, or it might have been concocted for him:

> 54. I, Thomas of Woodstock, the eighth day of September, the twenty-first year of my lord the king, acknowledge that I incited other men to assent to the making of a commission, in which I with others restrained my lord of his freedom and took upon me with others royal power, truly not knowing nor understanding at that time, as I do now, that I acted against his estate and royalty. And as I afterwards knew I had done wrong, and had taken upon myself more than I

ought to have done. I submitted myself to my lord and cried to him for mercy and grace, and still do, as lowly and meekly as a man may, and put myself high and low in his grace, as to him who has always been full of mercy and grace to all other men.

Also, as to the time that I came armed into my lord's presence and into his palace, even though I did it for dread of my life, I acknowledge for certain that I did evil against his regality and his estate: wherefore I submit myself in meek and lowly fashion to his mercy and his grace.

Also, in that I took my lord's letters from his messengers and opened them against his permission, I acknowledge that I did evil: wherefore I put myself lowly in his grace.

Also, in that I slandered my lord I acknowledge that I did evil and acted wickedly, in that I spoke it to him in slanderous fashion in the hearing of other folk. But by the way that my soul shall go, I did not mean any evil by this. Nevertheless, I know and acknowledge that I did evil and acted ignorantly: wherefore I submit myself high and low to his grace.

Also, in that I with others deliberated for fear of my life to give up my homage to my lord, I acknowledge well that with others I certainly talked to and asked certain clerks whether we might give up our homage for fear of our lives, or not. And whether we agreed to do that, truly and upon my oath I do not rightly remember, but I rather think we did: wherefore I submit myself high and low and evermore to his grace.

Also, in that I was in a place where discussion and conference took place about deposing my liege lord, truly I acknowledge well that we agreed to it for two or three days; and then we resumed our homage and our oaths and put him as high in his estate as he ever was. But indeed I acknowledge that I acted wrongly and unnaturally to him that is my liege lord, and has been so good and kind a lord to me. Wherefore notwithstanding my unnatural behavior I beseech him evermore to exercise his mercy and grace, as lowly as any creature may beseech it to his liege lord. [*Rolls of Parliament*, 1397]

Gloucester, Arundel and Warwick were appealed before parliament for accroaching the king's power, the same charge they had brought against their victims in 1388. Richard had, by now, mastered the art of manipulating parliaments. This one met at Westminster, and as its usual place, the Great Hall, was being renovated, it sat in a pavilion with open sides. From here, all had a good view of the king's archers who were surrounding them. Richard was later accused of influencing the sheriffs to return members favorable to him, and that may or may not have been true, but he certainly created a party of his own, which guided the rest. The Speaker, Sir John Bussy, was his man. During the trial, Arundel was to exclaim, "Where are the faithful Commons? The faithful Commons are not here!"

When the proceedings began, Gloucester was not present, for he had died in Calais Castle, perhaps from his illness, which seems to have been genuine, though perhaps not. In any event, his death was opportune, for it saved John of Gaunt the embarrassment of sitting in judgment on his brother. Warwick did not try to defend himself, but, "like a wretched old woman, made confession, wailing and weeping and whining that he had done all, traitor that he was, submitting himself in all things to the king's grace." He was sentenced to a traitor's death, but the king was so gratified at his humiliation that he commuted this to banishment to the Isle of Man. Arundel was executed, though his rank ensured it was done by beheading and not hanging, drawing and quartering. A surly, truculent man, he had given Richard extra cause to hate him by arriving late for the queen's funeral and then asking permission to leave early. Richard had struck him to the ground.

There remained the earls of Derby and Nottingham. Richard had won them over by promising to pardon them fully, and they had even joined those who appealed Gloucester, Arundel and Warwick. As a reward, Derby was made duke of Hereford while Nottingham was made duke of Norfolk. Once again, though,

CHAPTER 7. RICHARD II OF ENGLAND

Richard was only biding his time. He did not have long to wait. In January 1398, Hereford delivered the following document to the king in Parliament:

> 55. Sire, in the month of December, in the twenty-first year of your reign, as the duke of Hereford was riding between Brentford and London, the duke of Norfolk overtook him in great haste and spoke to him on divers matters, among which he said, "We are about to be undone."
>
> And the duke of Hereford asked, "Why?"
>
> And he replied that it was for the deed of Radcot Bridge. And the duke of Hereford said, "How should this be, for he pardoned us, and made declaration for us in Parliament, saying that we have been good and loyal towards him?"
>
> And the duke of Norfolk replied, "Notwithstanding this, it will be done with us as it has been done with others before, for he wishes to annul this record." And the duke of Hereford said that it would be a great marvel, since the king had said it before people, that it should afterwards be annulled.
>
> The duke of Norfolk said further that it was a wondrous world and false. "For I know full well," said he, "that if it had not been for some persons, my lord your father of Lancaster and you would have been seized and slain."
>
> The duke of Hereford said he knew well that the king had sworn by St. Edward to be a good lord to him. The duke of Norfolk answered, saying that so had he done to him many times, on the Body of Christ, and in spite of that he did not trust him the better. [*Rolls of Parliament*, 1398]

Norfolk denied the accusation and, as there were no witnesses, the only way to resolve the question was trial by battle. The duel was to take place at Coventry, in September 1398, an event which, with its elaborate ritual, promised to be as spectacular as it was exciting. When all was ready, though, Richard, to the fury of the spectators, refused to let the fight take place. His reasons are obscure, but it is possible that he could not bear the thought of either man winning. His solution was to banish Hereford for ten years and Norfolk for life.

Richard's successes seem to have made him reckless, and there were signs, too, of paranoia and megalomania. Moreover, he was, as usual, short of money. Two chroniclers describe his behavior at this time:

> 56. The king on solemn days, when he was accustomed to celebrate them regally, ordered a throne to be prepared, where he was wont to sit after supper until vespers, speaking to none, but looking at all. And when he glanced at anyone, no matter their rank, that person had to bend the knee in obeisance.
>
> Then the king called together his councilors and the archbishops and bishops at Nottingham, and said that he could not safely ride through the kingdom on account of the hatred of the men of London and the seventeen adjacent shires, and therefore he would destroy them with an army that he would assemble unless they would find him a pledge of good behavior. Therefore they ordered that the city and each shire should collect a great sum of money and offer it to him as a pledge of peace, and this was done. They ordered moreover that archbishops, bishops, abbots, priors, lords and commons in the cities and towns should affix blank charters in which the king intended later on, as it is said, to write this sentence. "As we have gravely offended your majesty in days gone by, we give ourselves and our goods to you, at the promptings of your will." [*Continuatio Eulogii Historiarum*]

[Note: The purpose of the blank charters was, in fact, not known, but the people who had been forced to seal them must have lived in fear.]

> 57. The king took as a loan great sums of money from many lords, both spiritual and temporal, and other persons in the realm promising to them under letters patent [open letters from the king], that he would repay these borrowed sums

within a limited period, but he never returned them to the creditors.

The king, desiring to subdue and oppress the people of his realm, directed letters patent to all shires of his realm, and induced them by terror, both clerical and lay subjects, to swear unaccustomed oaths of a kind which could really cause the final destruction of his people, and forced his subjects to confirm these oaths under their letters and seals.

Moreover, he made the sheriffs throughout the realm swear unaccustomed oaths, that they should obey all the king's commands, whether they were directed to them under the Great or the Privy Seal, and also letters directed to them under the signet. And if the sheriffs should know of any of his bailiffs, of whatever condition they were, who should utter or speak any evil, publicly or privately, in dishonor or disgrace of the king's person, they should imprison them, until they should receive orders from the king. From this it happened that many of his lieges were maliciously accused of saying something, either publicly or in secret, which could turn to the slander, disgrace, or dishonor of the king's person; and they were taken and imprisoned and led before the constable and marshal of England in the Court of Chivalry. And they were not exonerated until they had defended and acquitted themselves personally in single combat, notwithstanding the fact that their accusers and appealers were strong and healthy young men, whereas those who were accused were mostly weak, maimed and infirm. This was not only a great destruction of the realm, but struck fear into all members of the community. [Thomas of Walsingham, *History of England*, 1399]

John of Gaunt had made no protest against the arrest and death of his brother, or the banishment of his eldest son. However, he died early in 1399. Hereford now became duke of Lancaster, and, potentially, the most powerful man in England. Richard felt he could not allow him to return, so he extended his banishment to one for life and confiscated his vast estates. At the time of his banishment Hereford had been given letters patent guaranteeing his inheritance, but it was now decreed that they had been granted "by inadvertence and without suitable advice or proper deliberation." There was now general alarm, for if the king was capable of confiscating the Lancaster estates, then none was safe.

At this critical moment an Irish chieftain, Art McMurrough, rebelled. Richard would have done best to ignore McMurrough, but he decided, instead, to lead an army into Ireland. It landed at Waterford on 1 June. Wild rumors now spread that Richard intended to make Ireland his base, from where he would despoil England. Many nobles were to be killed and their estates confiscated. Lancaster, an intelligent, determined man, realized his chance had come. He landed at Ravenspur, on the Humber, and made his way to his family stronghold of Pontefract. He was joined by the most powerful men in the north, the earl of Northumberland, his son Henry Hotspur and the earl of Westmorland.

Richard now hastened from Ireland but due partly to incompetence and partly to treachery his army melted away. In the end, he took refuge in Conway Castle, which he was persuaded to leave by trickery and false promises. He was then taken to the Tower of London, where he had an interview with Lancaster:

> 58. The king asked the duke of Lancaster, "Why do you keep me so closely guarded by your men-at-arms? I wish to know if you acknowledge me as your lord and king, or what you mean to do with me."
>
> The duke replied, "It is true you are my lord and king, but the Council of the Realm has ordered that you should be kept in confinement until the day of the meeting of Parliament."
>
> Then was the king in great wrath, but he could not help himself, and said to the duke, that he did great wrong, both to him and the Crown. The duke replied, "My lord, we cannot do otherwise till the Parliament meets."
>
> The king was so enraged by this speech that he could scarcely speak, and paced twenty-three steps down the room without uttering a word; and presently he broke out thus,

CHAPTER 7. RICHARD II OF ENGLAND

"You have acknowledged me as your king these twenty-two years, how dare you use me so cruelly? I say that you behave to me like false men and like false traitors to their lord; and this I will prove, and fight four of the best of you, and this is my pledge"; saying which the king threw down his bonnet.

The duke of Lancaster fell on his knees, and besought him to be quiet till the meeting of Parliament, and there everyone would bring forward his reason.

"At least, fair sirs, for God's sake let me be brought to trial, that I may give an account of my conduct, and that I may answer to all they would say against me."

Then said the duke of Lancaster, "My lord, be not afraid, nothing unreasonable shall be done to you." And he took leave of the king, and not a lord who was there durst utter a word. [*Chronicle of the Treason and Death of Richard II*]

Lancaster was determined to depose Richard and make himself king. There was a precedent, since Richard's great-grandfather, Edward II, had been deposed in 1327. Four things were necessary. The first was that the king should abdicate voluntarily. Secondly, some sort of representative assembly must receive the act of abdication. Thirdly, a catalogue of the king's misdeeds must be submitted to the assembly, so that it could decide that the king deserved to be deposed, and formally depose him. Finally, a successor must be installed.

Richard had shown no signs of wanting to relinquish the crown, so he was kept incarcerated and the following account was prepared of the interview in the Tower:

59. The duke of Lancaster, and also the archbishop of Canterbury, came into the king's presence in the Tower, many others being present. And after the king had spoken apart with the duke and the archbishop, looking from one to the other with a cheerful countenance, as it seemed to the bystanders, calling all those present to him, declared publicly that he was ready to make the renunciation and resignation according to his promise.

And immediately he added to the aforesaid renunciation and cession, that if it were in his power the duke of Lancaster should succeed him in the realm. But because this was in no wise in his power, he asked the archbishop of York and the bishop of Hereford to declare and intimate his renunciation and cession to all the estates of the realm, to declare his intention and wish in this matter to the people. And as a token of his wish, he took off his finger the gold ring with his signet, and put it on the duke's finger. [*Rolls of Parliament,* 1399]

The assembly which was to depose Richard could not be a parliament, as there was no parliament without the king. Instead, members were summoned as for a parliament, a crowd was invited from the city of London and the resulting assembly was given the name of the "estates of the realm." It was an institution with no legal standing but, undeterred, it proceeded with the deposition:

60. In the great hall at Westminster, in the place honorably prepared for holding parliament, the archbishops of Canterbury and York and the duke of Lancaster, and other dukes, and lords both spiritual and temporal, and a great multitude of the people of the realm being gathered there, the duke of Lancaster occupying his usual and proper place, and the royal throne, solemnly prepared with cloth of gold being vacant, the archbishop of York and the bishop of Hereford publicly declared the cession and renunciation to have been made by the king. And at once the archbishop of Canterbury asked the estates of the people then present, whether they wished to accept the renunciation and cession for their interests and the good of the realm. The estates and people considering that it would be very expedient, each one singly, and then in common with the people, unanimously and cordially gave his consent.

After this acceptance it was publicly set forth that it would be advantageous for the kingdom, to avoid all scruple and evil suspicion, that the many crimes and defects frequently

committed by the king in the bad government of the realm
might be declared to the people. [Ibid.]

A document containing thirty-three indictments was now read.
It included the following:

61. The king refused to keep and defend the just laws and
customs of the realm, but according to the whim of his desire he wanted to do whatever appealed to his wishes. Sometimes, and often when the laws of the realm had been declared and expressed to him by the justices and others of his
council and he should have done justice to those who sought
it according to those laws, he said expressly, with harsh and
determined looks, that the laws were in his own mouth;
sometimes he said that they were in his breast, and that he
alone could change or establish the laws of his realm.

In many great councils of the king, when the lords of the
realm, the justices and others were charged faithfully to
counsel the king in matters touching the estate of himself
and the realm, often the lords, justices and others when they
were giving their advice, were suddenly and sharply rebuked
by him, so that they did not dare to speak the truth about
the state of the king and kingdom in giving their advice.

Although the lands and tenements, goods and chattels of
every freeman, according to the laws of the realm used
through all past times, ought not to be seized unless they
have been lawfully forfeited; nevertheless the king, propos-
ing and determining to undo such laws, declared that the
lives of every one of his lieges and their lands, tenements,
goods and chattels are his at his pleasure which is entirely
against the laws and customs of the realm. [Ibid.]

The deposition of the king followed:

62. It seemed to all the estates who were interrogated thereupon, that those accusations of crime and defaults were sufficient and notorious enough for the deposition of the king.
Whereupon all estates unanimously agreed that there was

abundant reason for proceeding to deposition, for the greater
security and tranquillity of the realm and the good of the
kingdom. Therefore the estates and communities deputed
certain commissioners to carry out this sentence of deposition and to depose King Richard from all his royal dignity,
majesty, and honor, on behalf of, in the name of, and by
authority of, all the estates, as has been observed in similar
cases by ancient custom of the realm. [Ibid.]

So far, the proceedings had followed those of the deposition of
Edward II, but now there was a problem, because Edward had been
succeeded by his son, the legitimate heir. Richard II had no children and his heir was the earl of March, a boy of eight. Lancaster
had no intention of stepping down for a child. In private discussions with his followers, the duke had wanted to resurrect a fanciful claim that his ancestor, Edmund Crouchback, had been the
eldest son of Henry III, but that would have meant that the four
Plantagenet monarchs who had ruled since 1272 had all been up-
starts. Lancaster had also suggested he should claim the throne by
right of conquest, but it was pointed out that this would cost him
the trust of his subjects, since a conqueror is under no obligation
to respect lives and property. At length, a compromise had been
reached. The ceremony continued:

63. And at once it being manifest that the realm of England
was vacant, Henry duke of Lancaster, rising in his place,
and standing erect so that he might be seen by the people,
and humbly making the sign of the cross on his forehead
and his breast, and invoking the name of Christ, claimed
the realm of England in his mother tongue in the following
words:
"In the name of the Father, Son and Holy Ghost, I, Henry
of Lancaster, challenge this realm of England and the crown
with all its members and appurtenances, as I am descended
by right line of blood from the good lord King Henry III,
and through that right that God of His grace has sent me,
with the help of my kindred and friends to recover it; the

which realm was on the point of being undone for default of governance and undoing of good laws." [Ibid.]

After Lancaster had knelt and prayed, the two archbishops led him to the throne, amidst enthusiastic applause. The archbishop of Canterbury then preached a sermon on the text, "This same shall rule over my people" [1 Samuel 9:17], and Lancaster gave the following assurance:

> 64. Sires, I thank God and you lords spiritual and temporal and all the estates of the land; and let you know that it is not my will that any man should think that by way of conquest I would disinherit any man of his heritage, franchise, or other rights he ought to have, nor put him out of what he has and has had by the good laws and customs of the realm; except those persons who have been against the good purpose and the profit of the realm. [Ibid.]

The following day, sentence was pronounced:

> 65. It is ordered by all the prelates, by all lords of the council, and by the commons of England that Richard, king of England, be sentenced and condemned to be imprisoned in a royal castle; that he have the best bread and the best meat that can be found for gold or silver; and if any should raise war for his deliverance he should be the first that should suffer death. [*Chronicle of the Treason and Death of Richard II*]

Richard was taken to Pontefract Castle. In 1400, there was a rising in his favor, and Henry sent a knight to murder him. His body was displayed in London for two days, so that all could see he was dead.

Richard II's story seems to cast doubts on the value of political theory. Issues were decided by naked force, and then theories were invented to justify actions. But in politics, as in sport, the game is spoiled if players do not obey the rules. The rule of law received two hammer blows, one from Richard II, who became a tyrant, and one from Henry of Lancaster, who usurped the throne. The charade of Richard's deposition fooled no-one. Henry was a usurper, so it followed that since he had deposed Richard, others could depose him. He had to watch his back for as long as he lived and, indeed, there was feudal anarchy in England for much of the fifteenth century. It was left to the Tudors, in the sixteenth century, to restore stability with the aid of the middle classes.

However, the doctrine of the supremacy of the law survived both the disorders of the late Middle Ages, and the Tudor despotism of the sixteenth century. In the seventeenth century it was used to combat the Stuart theory of the divine right of kings, and in the eighteenth century it was to inspire the Constitution of the United States of America.

CHAPTER 8
CHIVALRY

THE IDEAL

The word "chivalry" comes from the French *chevalier*, or "horseman." It was sometimes used in the sense of "cavalry," but here it means a code of behavior for those who fought on horseback, that is, knights and nobles of all ranks. A Majorcan, Ramón Llull, describes the mythical origins of chivalry:

> 66. When kindness, loyalty, truth and justice vanished, cruelty, injury, disloyalty and falsehood arose. There was evil in the world in which God had made man to love, serve and honor Him. When the world lapsed into wickedness, it was fear which restored justice. And so the people were divided into groups of a thousand, and from each group one man was chosen who was the most loyal, most brave, most knowledgeable and most courteous of them all.
>
> After that, they looked for the most suitable animal, the most handsome, the bravest, the strongest, and the most fitting to serve this man. And they found that the horse was the noblest and most suitable to serve him. Because the horse was chosen rather than any other animal, the man takes the name of the horse, which is *cheval* in French, so the man is *chevalier*, or, in English, "knight." Thus the noblest man was given the noblest beast. After that, arms were chosen that were the best for war, and to protect this man from death. And these arms were given to the knight. [*The Book of the Order of Chivalry*, 1276]

A French nobleman, Geoffrey de Charny, describes the ceremony of making a knight:

67. First of all, he must confess, and repent, and then prepare to receive communion. Then, the day before he is to
be made a knight, he must take a bath, and remain there a
long time, thinking that he is washing his body clean of the
grime of sin and evil living, and leaving such grime in the
water. Then, with a clear conscience, he should leave the
bath and lie in a bed with clean, white sheets of linen, and
there he should take his ease, as one who has escaped from
the pain of sin and the danger of hell. The bed stands for the
peace that comes from goodness, and for his reconciliation
with God, for all that he has done in the past to anger Him.

Then the knights come to dress him. They ought to dress
him in new linen, in everything new, showing that as his
body is cleansed of sin, so he is clad anew in what is white
and pure, signifying that he should, from that time forth,
keep himself pure and free from sin. Then the knights ought
to clothe him in a red tunic, showing that he must shed blood
to defend the faith of God and the Holy Church. Then the

knights ought
to bring black
shoes, and put
them on him
to show that,
as he came
from earth, he
must return to
earth, and
must be ready
for death at
any time.
Then the
knights ought to bring him a white belt, and put it
around his body, showing than he must be enveloped in chastity and purity. Then the knights ought to bring him a red
mantle, and place it on his shoulders, for, in olden times,
mantles were a sign of true humility.

CHAPTER 8. CHIVALRY

Then the knights ought to lead him joyfully into the church, and he ought to remain in the church, keeping vigil until morning. He should pray to Our Lord to forgive him the wasted sleepings and wakings of the past, and beg for help that he will, henceforth, be vigilant in His service.

The next morning, the knights lead him to hear Mass, and pray to Our Lord for grace to enter His service. And when Mass has been sung, the knights lead him to the knight who is to bestow the order upon him. He gives two golden spurs to two other knights, who put them on the candidate's feet, to show that since gold is the most coveted of metals, it is placed on his feet, because his heart has lost all desire for it.

Then the knight who is to confer the order of chivalry takes a sword, because a sword cuts with two edges. The knight must uphold the true and the just everywhere, without going against the Christian faith and Holy Church. Then the knights should kiss him, to confirm that they bestow the order upon him, so that he may be full of peace, love and loyalty. Then the knights should slap him on the cheek, as a sign that he must always remember that he has received the order of chivalry, and act as that order requires. [*The Book of Chivalry*, c. 1350]

Of all the knightly qualities, courage was, perhaps, the most important. De Charny wrote:

68. You will often be afraid when you see your enemies charging you, their lances in rest to strike you and their swords drawn to attack you. Bolts and arrows fly at you and you do not know how to protect yourself. Now you see men slaying each other, fleeing, dying and being taken prisoner, while your friends' corpses lie before you. Your horses, though, are not dead, and you could escape. With them, you could save your life, and none would know. If you remain, you will be honored for ever more. If you escape, you will dishonor yourself. Is not this a terrible choice? [Ibid.]

An anonymous masterpiece, the *Chanson de Roland,* describes the Battle of Roncesvalles of 778. The work is almost pure fiction, but it does give a clear idea of how a knight was expected to conduct himself in battle. Obviously, the hero's rival must be a worthy opponent. This is the poet's description of the Moorish leader, the Emir Balignant:

69. The Emir puts on his coat of mail with its gilded skirts, laces his helmet, covered with jewels set in gold and then girds his sword. He calls it "Precieuse" and this word has become his battle cry. From his neck, he hangs a great shield, which has a golden boss and is bordered with crystal. His spear, which he calls "Maltet," has a shaft as thick as a club, and a head heavy enough to make a load for a pack mule. Then he mounts his horse. He sits well in the saddle. He has narrow hips, but a deep chest, beautifully formed, and broad shoulders. He has a proud face, while his hair is curled and as white as any flower of summer. He has proved his bravery many times. Dear God, what a knight he would make, if only he were a Christian!

[Balignant and the Emperor Charlemagne meet in battle.]

The emir shouts "Precieuse!" and Charles his own famous battle cry, "Mountjoy!" The two men recognize each other and charge. Each one's spear smashes through the other's shield, but neither is wounded. The girths snap, the saddles tilt and both kings fall to the ground. They at once jump to their feet and draw their swords. They rain heavy blows on the shields, cutting them through and through until they fall in pieces. Then they assail the coats of mail and the sparks fly as they strike the helmets.

The emir is a skilled fighter. He strikes Charles's helmet of bright steel, cleaving it so that his sword slices flesh from his head and exposes the bone. Charles almost falls, but God does not will that he should be defeated or killed. St. Gabriel comes to him and says, "Mighty King, what is happening?" When he hears the angel's voice, Charles no longer fears death, and his strength returns. He strikes the emir with his sword, splits his helmet and, scattering his brains, cuts open his head down to his white beard.

Charles calls "Mountjoy!" The heathen flee, for it was not God's will that they should prevail. The French have the victory for which they longed. [*Chanson de Roland*]

However, far more than courage was required. Ramón Llull describes the duties of a knight:

70. The duty of a knight is to defend the holy Catholic faith, according to which God the Father sent His Son into the world, and was made flesh in the glorious Virgin, Our Lady Mary. As Our Lord has chosen clerics to maintain the holy Catholic faith against unbelievers, using Scripture and reason, so our glorious God has chosen knights to vanquish those unbelievers who strive to destroy Holy Church by force of arms.

The duty of the knight is to support and defend his earthly lord in administering justice. Knights should uphold justice, for as it is the duty of judges to judge, so it is the duty of knights to protect them from violence. If knights could become learned in the law, none would be better suited to hold the office of judge.

Knights should joust on their chargers, and take part in tournaments. They should hunt deer, boars and other wild animals, for in doing such things, they exercise their skill in arms, so that they are more able to carry out their duties as knights. And as a knight should exercise his body, so he should practice justice, wisdom, charity, loyalty, truth, humility and hope, so that he may perfect his soul.

The duty of a knight is to protect women, widows, orphans and men who are in trouble and cannot help themselves. To wrong women and widows who are in need of help, and orphans who are in need of support, and rob and destroy the weak, are all against the rules of chivalry. It is a great evil, when a knight indulges in such wickedness, for he is acting against loyalty, justice and, above all, the noble order of chivalry.

As God has given eyes to craftsmen so that they may see their work, so he has given eyes to sinners, that they may weep for their sins. And as God has given a knight a brave and noble heart, so it should be a heart full of mercy. His heart should lead him to deeds of humanity and pity. He should help all who, in sorrow, beg aid and mercy from knights and who put their trust in them. [*The Book of the Order of Chivalry,* 1276]

The suggestion that knights might study law is unusual. The notion of a fighting judge is rather alarming, but, not only that, a knight was not expected to have much book learning. He had indeed to be highly educated, but only in the art of war and kindred skills, such as riding, hunting and jousting. Knights of the early Middle Ages disdained reading and writing, which was for clerics, but that, at least, was to change in later centuries. Llull himself was quite clear about the differences between the education of clerics and knights:

71. Clerks study doctrine that they may know God, love Him and teach the common herd that they, too, may know, love, serve and honor Him. To gain this learning, they attend schools. As clerks, by the example of their honesty and learning, guide the people into the paths of righteousness, so knights, by their nobility and force of arms, strike such fear into the common folk that they deter them from wronging each other.

As for schooling in chivalry, a knight should have his son taught to ride when young, for he will not learn when he is old. The son of the knight, while he is a squire, should learn how to care for horses. He should also learn how to serve, before he becomes a lord, or he would not understand how noble is the authority of a knight. Therefore, every man who wishes to become a knight, should learn how to serve, arm, and equip one, and learn also how to carve at table. [Ibid.]

The distinction between knights and ordinary folk was even clearer:

72. It is right that the common people should cultivate the land and produce fruits and goods to maintain the knight and his horses. And a knight should lead a life that is in keeping with his status, exercising himself by hunting and enjoying those things which others provide him with their labor. [Ibid.]

73. A knight must not cultivate the soil, or tend vines, or keep beasts, and he must not be a shepherd or a lawyer. And when he is serving as a soldier, he must not buy lands or vineyards, and if he should buy, then the property is his lord's. The reason is, that knights must not be tempted to forsake arms for earthly riches. [Honoré Bonet, *The Tree of Battles*, 1387]

A knight must know how to obey, as well as command:

74. Above all, a knight must keep the oath which he has taken to his lord. A knight is not true, who, through fear of death or any other reason, fails to defend his lord's land; indeed, he is a traitor. A knight must obey his lord, the captain of the host, and if he does not do so, he is not a worthy knight, but is arrogant and insolent. A knight should devote himself to gaining skill in arms, and fighting for his lord. He must always obey his lord's commands, and if he does not, he must lose his head. [Ibid.]

Sir Thomas Malory, the fifteenth-century writer of Arthurian romances, put these words into the mouth of Sir Ector de Maris, lamenting over his brother, Sir Lancelot:

75. Thou wert the courteoust knight that ever bare shield and thou wert the truest friend to thy lover that ever bestrad horse, and thou wert the truest lover of a sinful man that ever loved woman, and thou wert the kindest man that ever struck with sword, and thou wert the goodliest person that ever came among press of knights, and thou wert the meekest man that ever ate in hall among ladies, and thou wert the sternest knight to thy mortal foe that ever put spear in the rest. [*Morte d'Arthur,* xxi, 13]

Two of Chaucer's Canterbury Pilgrims were a knight and a squire:

76. A knight there was, and he a worthy man,
Who from the very time that he began
To ride abroad, had much loved chivalry,
Truth and honor, freedom and courtesy.
Full valiant was he in his liege lord's war,
And boldly had he ridden, no man more
In Christian and in heathen lands, I guess,
And ever honored for his worthiness.
Great Alexander's city he saw won;
He took the honoured place when he upon
The board sat with the knights of Prussia.
In Latvia he'd fought and in Russia,
More oft than Christian men of his degree.
And in Grenada at the siege was he
Of Agadir, and Benmarin as well,
And Ayas and Attalia when they fell.
Far all around the Great Sea arms he bore,
With forces storming many a distant shore.
In mortal battles had he been fifteen,
And fought for the true faith in Tramassene

CHAPTER 8. CHIVALRY

Thrice in the lists and always slew his foe.
This most courageous knight had been also
Campaigning with the lord of Palatie
Against another heathen in Turkey;
And evermore he bore away the prize.
But though he was so worthy, he was wise,
And in his bearing modest as a maid.
No villain thing he did, nor slander said
In all his life, but to all men was right.
He was a very perfect, gentle knight.
But let me tell you now of his array.
His horse was good, though he made no display.
His fustian tunic was all stained with rust
That from his hauberk rubbed, for he had just
Returnéd home from making his voyage
And joined with us to go on pilgrimage.
With him there was his son, a youthful squire,
A lover and a lusty lad of fire,
With locks so curled as if formed in a press.
Of twenty years he was, or maybe less.
To call him tall would certainly be wrong,
But he was active and immensely strong.
He had seen service with the cavalry
In Flanders, in Artois and Picardy
And fought full well, and in a little space
Of time, so he could win his lady's grace.
Decked out was he, just like a meadow bright
In bloom with lovely flowers, red and white.
Singing he was, and whistling all the day;
He was as fresh as is the month of May.
Short was his gown, with sleeves both long and wide.
Well did he sit his horse and fairly ride.
He could make songs, he knew how to indite,
To joust and dance, and poetry could write.
So hot he loved, and here I tell no tale,
He slept no more than does the nightingale.

> Courteous he was, meek and serviceable
> And carved before his father at table.
> [*The Canterbury Tales,* General Prologue, 11. 43-100]

Chaucer divides the knightly qualities between father and son. It was not enough that a knight should fight valiantly in many wars, but that the adventures should be far-flung. This man has done battle all along the frontiers of Christendom, smiting the infidel wherever he could be found. Curiously, though, he was willing to serve one Moslem against another. The knight is modest and he shows it by dressing simply, which was a great deal to ask of a gentleman of the late fourteenth century.

Fictional knights were the heroes of medieval romances, so they were as handsome as Hollywood heroes. The squire has this attribute. He is also madly, but honorably, in love with a lady who is, no doubt, of exquisite beauty and impeccable virtue. The strength of her affection for him will be in direct proportion to the number of men he can slay in battle. It seems that he has made a good start. Their love will culminate in marriage, and they will produce children as beautiful and as virtuous as themselves.

We are now in the late Middle Ages, so the squire has some civilized accomplishments which, in earlier times, would have been scorned. No man who was versed in the art of war alone would have been welcome at the court of Richard ii.

Though restraint in the choice of clothes might be desirable, it should not be carried too far. This is from a French book of stories for the use of preachers:

> 77. I have heard how, when a certain covetous knight ate at the court of a certain noble, and asked after dinner for his mantle, which his servant had laid among the other garments, then, seeing that it could not at once be found, he began to revile him before all that stood by, saying, "Son of a ___, bring my mantle forthwith! Knowest thou it not?"
>
> The servant, offended and moved to indignation, answered in all men's hearing, "Lord, I know it well, I have

known it these seven years past, yet I have not been able to find it." [Jacques de Vitry, *Examples,* c. 1230]

THE REALITY

We turn now from theory and fiction to reality. Here is an account of the squires of the English royal court in the fifteenth century:

78. There are 40 squires of the household, chosen according to their possessions, social positions and wisdom. Of these squires, 20 are always to be in this court, as attendants on the king, in riding and going at all times. They are also to help serve his table.

They eat in the hall, as they serve, some the first course, and some at the latter. Each of them takes at night half a gallon of ale. For the winter season, each takes two Paris candles and one faggot.

When any of them is present in court, he is allowed for daily wages 7½d, and his clothing, winter and summer, or else 40 shillings. They wear the king's livery, both for personal glory and for the proper worship of this honorable household. Each of them is to be allowed one honest servant in this court. If any of them be ill, he takes two loaves, two messes of the principal meat, and one gallon of ale for each day. They are also to have all the year, straw for their beds.

The squires are accustomed, afternoons and evenings, to gather in the lord's chamber. There they talk of chronicles of kings, pipe, harp, sing, or other martial arts, to help to occupy the court. [*Harleian Manuscripts,* British Museum]

This is an indenture made in 1374 between John of Gaunt and a squire. It will be remembered that Gaunt claimed the throne of Castile:

79. This indenture, made between our lord King John of Castile of the one part and Symkyn Molyneux, esquire, of the other part, witnesses that the said Symkyn is retained and will remain with our said lord for peace and for war for

the term of his life, as follows: that is to say, the said Symkyn shall be bound to serve our said lord as well in time of peace as of war in whatsoever parts it shall please our said lord, well and fitly arrayed. And he shall be boarded as well in time of peace as of war. And he shall take for his fees by the year, as well in time of peace as of war, ten marks sterling from the issues of the duchy of Lancaster at the terms of Easter and Michaelmas by even portions yearly for the whole of his life. And, moreover, our lord has granted to him by the year in time of war five marks sterling by the hands of the treasurer for war. And his year of war shall begin the day when he shall move from his inn towards our said lord by letters which shall be sent to him thereof, and thenceforward he shall take wages; and he shall have fitting freightage for him, his men, horses, and other harness within reason, and in respect of his war horses taken and lost in the service of our said lord, and also in respect to prisoners and other profits of war taken or gained by him or any of his men, the said lord will do to him as to other squires of his rank.

Given at Bordeaux, February 15, 1374. [John of Gaunt, *Register*]

During a war in Spain in 1367 a small band of English knights was surprised by a large force of Spaniards. Most of the English huddled together for protection, but not Sir William Felton:

80. He very bravely charged among the enemy, on horseback, lance couched. Striking a Spaniard upon his floweremblazoned shield, he thrust through his heart his sharp blade of steel. Down to the ground he hurled him, in the sight of all the people. Like a man full of great courage he rushed upon them with drawn sword. The Spaniards followed him on all sides and threw spears at him. They slew his horse under him, but Sir William Felton defended himself stoutly on foot, like a lionhearted man. Albeit, his defense availed him little, for he was slain. God have mercy on him. [Chandos Herald, *Life of the Black Prince*]

CHAPTER 8. CHIVALRY

The following is an example of knightly behavior from the First Crusade. The hero, Baldwin, was to become king of Jerusalem in 1100:

81. Baldwin had been wounded in battle while he rescued a foot soldier of his army, with whose bravery he had been much delighted. The leech whom he summoned feared in his foresight lest the cataplasm outwardly applied might film over the wound, which, as he knew, had pierced deep into the prince's body. He feared therefore lest, while the skin grew smooth over the wound, it might rankle inwardly with a mass of putrid matter. This he foresaw in his wondrous skill, partly by the most praiseworthy conjecture, and partly from past experience. He therefore besought the king to command that one of the Saracen prisoners (for it would have been wicked to ask it of a Christian) should be wounded in the same place, and afterwards slain; whereby he might inquire at better leisure in the dead man's body, nay might clearly discover from its examination, how it was with the king's wound at the very bottom. From this, however, the prince's loving kindness shrank in horror; and he repeated the ancient example of the Emperor Constantine, who utterly refused to become the cause of any man's death, even of the basest, for so small a chance of his own safety.

Then said the doctor, "If indeed thou art resolved to take no man's life for the sake of thine own cure, then at least send for a bear, a beast that is of no use but to be baited. Let him stand erect on his hinder paws with his fore-feet raised, and bid them thrust him with the steel then, by inspection of his bowels after death, I may in some degree measure how deep that wound is, and how deep thine own."

Then said the king, "We will not object to the beast, if need be. Do therefore as thou wilt." Whereupon it was done as the leech bade; and he discovered from this proof of the wild beast how perilous it would have been for the king if the lips of the wound had become united before the matter had been drawn forth and the bottom had grown together.

Let this suffice concerning the king's mercy. [Guibert of Nogent, *God's Dealings*]

A man who was said to exemplify all the knightly virtues was Edward, the Black Prince (1330-1376), eldest son of King Edward III:

82. He was sober in his actions, but his sword was often drunk with the blood of the enemy. Harshly attacking his foes, he fought and defeated them. His sword point refused to go back into the sheath dry. His hostile blade was sated with enemy gore. A torrent of blood slaked the thirst of his weapons. His broadsword was unwilling to sleep within the scabbard; it disgorged itself out of its mouth. [John Gower, *Vox Clamantis*]

In 1356, the prince commanded the English army which defeated the French at Poitiers. During the battle, King John of France was captured, along with many nobles and lesser men:

83. The same day of the battle at night the prince made a supper in his lodgings for the French king and for the most part of the great lords who were prisoners. The prince made the king and his son, the lord James of Bourbon, the lord John of Artois, the count of Artois, the count of Joinville, and the lord of Partenay to sit all at one board, and other lords, knights and squires at other tables; and always the prince served before the king as humbly as he could, and would not sit at the king's board for any desire that the king could make, but said he was not sufficient to sit at the table with so great a prince as the king.

Then the prince said to the king, "Sir, for God's sake, think no evil and be not dismayed, though God this day did not consent to follow your will; for, sir, surely the king my father shall bear you as much honor and friendship as he can possibly do, and shall agree with you so reasonably that you shall ever be friends together hereafter. And, sir, methinks you ought to rejoice, though the day did not go as you would have it. For this day you have won the high renown of prowess and you have surpassed this day in valor all others of your party. Sir, I say this not to mock you, for all that are on our side, that saw every man's deeds, are plainly agreed to give you the prize and crown."

Therewith the Frenchmen began to whisper and said among themselves how the prince had spoken nobly, and that by all estimation he should prove a noble man, if God should send him life and allow him to persevere in such good fortune. [Jean Froissart, *Chronicles*]

The people of Limoges must have had a different opinion of the Black Prince. Froissart describes the siege of 1370:

84. The prince was before the city of Limoges for about a month. There was no assault, but daily they mined. And they within made a countermine to destroy the English miners, but they failed. And when the prince's miners saw how the countermines against them failed, they said to the prince, "Sire, whenever it shall please you, we shall cause a part of the wall to fall into the ditch. Then you shall be able to enter the city without any danger."

These words greatly pleased the prince who said, "Do it tomorrow."

Then the miners set fire into their mine [to burn away the timbers that were supporting the roof], and so the next morning a great length of the wall fell down and filled the ditches. At this, the English were glad. Some of their footmen entered the town with ease and ran to the gate and beat down the barriers, for there was no defense against them. It was done so suddenly that they of the town did not know what was happening.

Then all the other footmen entered the city, ready to plunder it and to slay men, women and children, which they were ordered to do. It was great pity to see the men, women and children that kneeled before the prince for mercy. But he was so angry, that he took no notice of them, and all were put to death, though they were not guilty of anything. There was no pity taken on the poor people who had done no treason, yet they suffered more than the important men who had done evil. There was not so hard a heart within the city of Limoges, if he had any remembrance of God, but that wept piteously for the great mischief that they saw before their eyes; for more than 3,000 men, women and children were slain and beheaded that day. God have mercy on their souls, for they were martyrs. [Ibid.]

During the massacre, the Black Prince came upon three French knights who were resisting bravely. After watching them fight for a while, he ordered that their lives should be spared. It was said that he admired their courage, but he must also have considered that knights who were taken prisoner paid ransoms, while humble folk did not.

IDEAL MEETS REALITY: THE JUST WAR

A fundamental question for knights was whether it was right for them to kill at all, though most must have resolved this to their own satisfaction at least, or they would have followed an alternative career, probably the church. But under what circumstances was it right to kill?

It was generally agreed that a just war needed to fulfill three conditions. In the first place it had to be authorized by a legitimate ruler. Individuals should not start a war on their own initiative. Secondly, the cause must be just, for example the defense of the realm or the redress of a wrong. Wars were not just if they were fought for gain or out of malice. Thirdly, the ultimate objective must be a lasting peace. If a knight was sure all these conditions were met, then it was his duty to take part in the war. But how could he be sure, and, if he had doubts, what of his oaths to his overlord? Disobedience was a sin, as was killing in an unjust war.

Sometimes there was clear and unequivocal advice. Gratian of Bologna, a twelfth-century Camaldolese monk and canon lawyer, quotes this letter which Pope Urban II (1088-1099) wrote to the bishop of Gap:

85. Prohibit those soldiers who have sworn fealty to Count Hugh from serving him. Let them be forewarned that if they reach out to the sacraments that they ought to serve God rather than men [Acts 5:25]. For no authority binds them to fulfill the fealty they have sworn to a Christian prince who is now the enemy of God and His saints, and who tramples upon their commands. [*Decretum of Canon Law*, 1159]

There were, though, many knights who would ignore such a decree, even at the risk of excommunication. Moreover, such specific guidance was usually lacking, so that men had to make their own decisions. The following extracts show how complicated the issue was. Stephen Langton, archbishop of Canterbury in the early thirteenth century, was obviously confused:

86. Item. [Suppose] the king of France is waging an unjust war against the king of England, and I am his [the king of France's] soldier. He, I know, calls on me so that I come to his aid. If I come, I sin, since I am obeying him in things that are against the precepts of God. If I don't come, I cause a scandal and I publicize his guilt, which is against the Gospel. What should this person do here?

In this case it is probable that there will be no scandal from his withdrawal from service; but if everyone withdraws, it would cause a scandal and would thus publicize [the king's] guilt. Some of them are obligated to withdraw, since no one of them causes a scandal from his own withdrawal; therefore all are obligated to withdraw from him. But if all of them withdraw, they cause a scandal and publicize [the king's] guilt; therefore they all cause a scandal, and therefore no one individual produces a scandal. Whose sin would this scandal be therefore, and who would be answerable to him, when no one of them has offended him?

I respond. In the first case, I come when I am called, but once I've arrived either I withdraw [from combat] or, remaining there, I do not use my arms. In the second case no one person causes a scandal; and yet everyone causes a scandal; and this is the key word: "everyone."

Item. A priest is not bound to give the Eucharist in private to one whom he knows is in mortal sin; but if he sins in public, he is bound to give it. By the same reasoning a knight who is bound to a king by an oath of fealty who knows that the king is attacking another prince unjustly, is not bound to aid him in private matters, but is bound to do so in public ones. When it has come to the point that the king is alone with the knight and here are ten or twenty on the opposing side, will this knight not be a traitor if he avoids the danger to the king and denies him aid?

When he knows that his cause is unjust, should he leave him alone in such great peril? We say that in battles there can be two kinds of actions: offense and defense. If the knight aids the king in attacking an enemy who has a just cause, he does evil. But if he aids his king in defense, no sin comes from this. [*Questions*]

A contemporary of Langton's, Robert of Courson, taught theology at the University of Paris and was also a crusader. He had this advice for those who scrupled to fight in an unjust war:

87. If the knights know for certain that a war is unjust, or that it is partly just or partly unjust, they should not follow the battle standard of the lord king. Indeed, in that case they may follow a middle course, namely, so that they neither incur confiscation of their temporal goods nor are disinherited, but neither do they follow their lord in burning down churches and other evil deeds.

The middle course is the one that the Lord gave to men in such a situation from the beginning all the way to the end of the world, namely that they take up the cross and go off in defense of the Holy Land. [*Summa*]

An Italian Dominican friar, Roland of Cremona, wrote:

88. If some of a king's people know that the king is attacking a city out of evil motives and that he does not have the right to attack it, and despite this some of the people believe that this fact might be hidden and that others do not

know that he is attacking unjustly, then it appears to me that some of the people who do believe this to be the case should [still] follow the king.

Nevertheless, those people should do less on that expedition than they could. Why do I say this? Because some of the people who hold this view are still bound to go, like a judge who knows the truth of a case and has the contrary sufficiently proven to him and nevertheless condemns an innocent person. If, however, it is known publicly to all the people that the king is attacking unjustly, then these people are obligated not to follow him, even if the king is bound to kill them, since "Obedience to God comes before obedience to men."

What if the king starts that war on the counsel of the princes who usually advise him, or the podestà on the advice of the council, and the king's council, or the podestà's council say that it should be started and that it is just? We then say that this portion of the people is able to go without sin, since they probably think, "There is some hidden information that I do not know," however much they believe that they know the facts of the matter well. And I say that none of the people can so know without that doubt rising in them, unless it had been revealed to them by the Holy Spirit that the advice of the princes or of the podestà is not right. And if it were revealed to them they are bound not to go, since then they know that the Lord does not want them to go, from what was revealed to them that that advice was evil.

To what Augustine says, that "the just war is that waged by the authority of the prince," we say that that saying should be understood in this way, that is: in as far as the war is just it must be waged by the authority of a prince, but this is not good enough, since many other things are also necessary. [Master Roland of Cremona, *Summa*, c. 1230]

It is hard to know what the average knight would have made of all this, but two points emerge. The door was at least partly opened for the conscientious objector; and that stock excuse of the perpetrator of atrocities, "I only obeyed orders," was undermined.

CHAPTER 9
JOUSTING, HUNTING
AND THE DUEL

IN THE CASTLE of Segovia, Spain, there are several small suits of armor, once worn by young boys. They were not given to the youngsters so that they could play war games, though no doubt they did, but to accustom them to walking and riding while encased in metal. Indeed, the most essential part of a knight's education was learning how to fight. Jousting in tournaments and hunting were an important part of this.

JOUSTING

One way the novice learnt how to handle a horse and a lance was by tilting at the quintain. This was like a weather vane, but with a target on one end and a loaded sack on the other. The horseman galloped at the quintain and tried to hit the target with his lance. If he succeeded, he then had to escape before the sack struck him from behind. The next stage was taking part in tournaments, which were combats with others like himself, and hunting, which was war to the death, albeit with four-legged enemies.

Before the thirteenth century, tournaments were mock battles and were fought without any rules, so that they often resulted in deaths and injuries. Jean de Marmoutier describes one such fracas, which took place in 1128:

89. A day was fixed for a tournament between the Normans and the Bretons. To help the Normans, there came William Clito, count of Flanders, Theobald, count of Blois, and his brother Stephen, later to be king of England. On the other side were the Bretons, lively enough, but few in numbers.

When Geoffrey saw how few the Bretons were, he left the stronger side and joined them. Then the battle began. There was the clash of arms, the braying of trumpets and horns, and the discordant neighing of horses.

Even the Mont-Saint-Michel glittered with sunbeams reflected from golden shields. The men fought as one. The shafts of their spears snapped and their swords broke. Men fell from their saddles, and riderless horses whinnied as they roamed aimlessly. Geoffrey, the terror of his enemies, rushed here and there, hurling his lances, waving his sword and killing many. Led by him, the Bretons followed, dealing death. Geoffrey pressed on, fighting like a lion, while the mass of the Bretons came forward, certain of victory. At last, the Normans wearied of the struggle and fled, the many routed by the few.

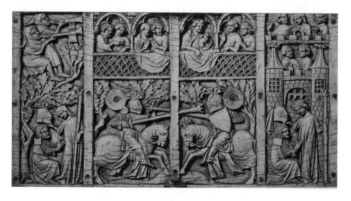

CHAPTER 9. JOUSTING & HUNTING

When news of this tournament had spread abroad, an enormous Saxon arrived whose strength and courage gave the Normans hope of victory. Far taller than any other man, he strode out from the Norman camp, taunted the Bretons, and dared them to send a man to fight him in single combat. Brave men turned pale, and lost their strength, fearing for anyone who would fight such a monster.

Geoffrey watched as brave men were paralyzed with fear as they were summoned. Then he bellowed with rage and rode to the fore. He took up his weapons, and, all eyes on him, he attacked the giant. The man had enormous strength, so that his lance pierced both the count's shield and his breastplate, wounding him badly. But Geoffrey was unmoved and, hurling his spear, he transfixed his foe. Then, standing over the fallen man, he cut off his head with his sword. [*Chronicles of the Counts of Anjou*]

Moslem Spain was more civilized than Christian Europe. This is an account of a tournament in Córdoba:

90. This day [21 April 975], the Caliph al-Hakam went on to the flat roof that overlooks the Azuda gate, accompanied by his son, Prince Abu-l-Walid. He wanted to watch a group of distinguished soldiers who had assembled for a tournament and see how they acquitted themselves on horseback, making mock attacks on each other. He also hoped the spectacle would amuse the prince.

He ordered the soldiers to take the greatest care not to hurt each other and that the blows they gave with their lances should be feints that would not cause wounds. He warned them to follow his instructions, threatening them with punishment if they disobeyed.

They then began the tournament with great enthusiasm, and there were various encounters, from which they emerged unscathed. They knocked each other down, taking great care not to inflict wounds. Nonetheless, Walid ibn 'Abd al-Malik ibn Musa ibn al-Tawil al-Tagri unintentionally attacked his adversary Masyan ibn al Jayr ibn Jazar, the Berber, with the point of his lance. He struck him between the shoulders and knocked him down so badly wounded that he had to be carried, dying, to his house. In the same way, Mundir ibn 'Abd Allah ibn Habil dealt his rival a similar blow.

The Caliph expressed his disapproval of these deeds, ordered that al-Walid and Mundir should be imprisoned and commanded them to send gifts to the wounded. [Isa ibn Ahmad al Eazi, *Annals of Caliph al-Hakam II of Córdoba*]

In England, Richard I made tournaments legal in 1194, though there were conditions. Each event needed a license from the king, it had to take place on an official tilting ground, and entrants had to pay fees according to their rank. Thus the king's knights not only received training, but contributed to his exchequer. Further, the king had control of a sport which could easily have lead to feuds between his more powerful subjects.

In the fourteenth and fifteenth centuries, tournaments developed rules and ceremonies. They were slightly safer, and were, moreover, magnificent spectacles, attracting large crowds. There were jousts between individuals while the mock battle survived as the mêlée.

Chaucer describes a mêlée:

91. The heralds leave their riding up and down,
Now ring out trumpets loud and clarion;
There is no more to say, but east and west
The threatening spears are falling into rest.
The sharp spurs penetrate the horses' side,
Now men see who can joust and who can ride.
Then shiver shafts on shields full strong and thick,
One through his breastbone feels the deadly prick.
Up spring the spears to twenty feet in height,
Out flash the swords, glinting like silver bright.
They smite the helms and hack and hew and shred.
Out bursts the blood in streams of deepest red.
The mighty maces smash the bones in twain,

One struggles through the press with might and main.
The noblest horses stumble, down goes all.
One rolls upon the ground as does ball,
But plies his mace as he regains his feet,
And from his horse he does his foe unseat.
One through his body's hurt and him they take
In spite of his resistance to the stake
Where the rules say he has now to abide;
He joins a lad that's from the other side.
From time to time lord Theseus makes them rest
To drink and be refreshed as they think best.
[*The Canterbury Tales,* The Knight's Tale, ll. 2599-2622]

This was a mêlée of another kind:

92. In the year 1214, Albizzo da Fiore was mayor of Padua, a prudent and discreet man, who was courteous, gentle and kindly, though he ruled with wisdom, dignity and skill, he nonetheless yet loved pleasure and recreation. During his period of office, there

was established at Treviso a Court of Solace and Mirth, where many people of Padua resorted, both knights and commoners. Moreover, a dozen of the noblest and fairest ladies that could be found in Padua were invited to grace that court.

Now the court, or festivity, was planned in this way. A fantastic castle was built and garrisoned with ladies and their waiting women, who, without any help from men defended it with all possible diligence. The castle was fortified on all sides with skins of vair and sable, sendals, purple cloths, samites, precious tissues, scarlet, brocade of Baghdad, and ermine. What shall I say of the golden coronets studded with chrysolites and jacinths, topaz and emeralds, pearls and pointed headgear, and all manner of adornments with which the ladies defended their heads from the onslaughts of the besiegers? For the castle was to be attacked, and the weapons and engines of war which the men used against it were apples and dates and muscat-nuts, tarts and pears and quinces, roses and lilies and violets, and vases of balsam or ambergris or rosewater, amber, camphor, cardamoms, cinnamon, cloves, pomegranates, and all kinds of flowers and spices that are fragrant to smell and good to see. Moreover, many men came from Venice to this festival, and many ladies to pay honor to that court; and these Venetians, bearing the fair banner of St. Mark, fought with great skill and pleasure.

Yet much evil may come from good beginnings, for while the Venetians struggled in sport with the Paduans, competing to be the first to force the castle gate, fighting broke out on both sides and (would it had never happened!) a foolish Venetian who was carrying the banner of St. Mark, fiercely attacked the Paduans. When the Paduans saw this, some of them became angry in their turn, and seized the banner, from which they tore a piece. This provoked the Venetians even more. So the court and the game were broken up on the orders of the stewards and of the Lord Paola of Sermendaula, who was then king of the knights at that court.

In the words of the poet, we might say, "The sport begat wild strife and anger; anger begat enmity and fatal war." For in the course of time, the hostility between Paduans and Venetians became so great that all trade between them was forbidden, and the frontiers were guarded to prevent goods being carried from one land to the other. Then men took to robbery and violence, so that there was even more discord, wars and deadly rivalry. [Roladino of Padua, *Chronicle*, 13th century]

The following is an account of a tournament at Smithfield near London in 1390, during the reign of Richard ii:

93. On the Sunday next after the feast of St. Michael, this feast and triumph were to begin, and that day were to take place at Smithfield the jousts called the Challenge. So the same Sunday, about three o'clock in the afternoon, there issued out of the Tower of London, first threescore coursers, ready for the jousts, and on every one a squire of honor, riding at an easy pace. Then issued out threescore ladies of honor, mounted on fair palfreys, riding on one side, richly appareled for the jousts; and every lady led a knight with a chain of silver, which knights were appareled to joust. Thus they came riding along the streets of London with a great many trumpeters and other minstrels, and so came to Smithfield, where the queen of England and other ladies and damsels were ready in chambers richly adorned to see the jousts, and the king was with the queen.

Thither came the earl of Saint Pol, nobly accompanied by knights and squires for the jousts which immediately commenced; and there jousted all the stranger [foreign] knights who wished to do so and had time before the night came on. Thus these jousts of challenge began and continued till it was dark. Then knights and ladies withdrew, and the queen was lodged beside St. Paul's in the bishop's palace, and there supper was prepared. The same evening the count of Ostervant came and was nobly received.

Now for these jousts on Sunday for the answerers without, the earl Walleran of Saint Pol had the prize and of the challengers, the earl of Huntingdon. There was goodly dancing in the queen's lodging in the presence of the king and his uncles and other barons of England and ladies and damsels, continuing till it was day.

On the next day, which was Monday, you might have seen in many places of the city of London, squires and varlets going about with harness and doing other business of their masters. After noon, King Richard came to the place all armed, richly appareled, accompanied with dukes, earls, lords and knights. The queen, well attended with ladies and damsels, came to the place where the jousts were to be, and mounted into chambers and scaffolds prepared for them. Then the earl of Ostervant, well attended by knights of his country, came into the field, and all were ready to joust.

Then the jousts began. Every man strove to obtain honor. Some were struck down from their horses. These jousts continued till it was nearly night. Then all people withdrew to their lodgings, and at the hour of supper went to court. There was a goodly supper, well prepared. For that day, the prize was given to the earl of Ostervant as the best jouster of the outer party, and well he deserved it. Of the inner party, a knight of England called Sir Hugh Spenser had the prize.

The next day, Tuesday, there were jousts again in the same place, by all manner of squires, which lasted till night. At supper, all men went to the bishop's palace, where the king, the queen and the ladies were. There was a good and costly supper, and afterward great dancing, continuing all night.

On Wednesday, they jousted in the same place, all manner of knights and squires who would joust. That was a sore and a rude joust, lasting till night. [This looks like a free-for-all. There is no mention of important spectators.]

On Thursday the king gave a supper to all knights and gentlemen strangers, and the queen to all ladies and damsels. Then on Friday the duke of Lancaster gave a dinner for all stranger knights and squires, which was a goodly dinner.

On Saturday the king and all the lords departed from London for Windsor. Then there began again great feasts, with dinners and suppers given by the king; and especially, the king did great honor to the earl of Ostervant, his cousin, who was requested by the king and his uncles to take on him the Order of the Garter. [Froissart, *Chronicles*]

Heralds had proclaimed the joust over much of Europe, but Froissart mentions only two distinguished foreign visitors. Both came from just over the water, Saint Pol from what is now northern France and Ostervant from Hainault, now part of Belgium. Moreover, both were from lands which belonged to Burgundy, a power friendly to England. Both won prizes!

FALCONRY

One of the most remarkable books of the Middle Ages is *On the Art of Hunting with Birds,* written by the emperor Frederick II of Hohenstaufen between 1244 and 1250.

Frederick had a scientific mind, something that was most unusual in his day. His spirit of inquiry led him to make experiments on live human beings, a tradition which his great admirer, Adolf Hitler, was to continue in the concentration camps; though, in fairness to Frederick, it must be mentioned that only a few individuals suffered at his hands, while he forbade the persecution of the Jews in his dominions. He devoted far more attention to his study of falconry, observing, experimenting and classifying in a way that would do credit to any modern ornithologist.

Frederick was so passionate about falconry that he took his hawks with him wherever he went and would hunt whenever he could, even if it meant neglecting such important duties as the conduct of a siege. Here he says why falconry is superior to any other kind of hunting:

> 94. By the proper use of falconry, birds of prey are taught to accept the company of humans, to fly after quarry and to behave exactly as they would in the wild. Anyone who merely plays at hunting can hold dogs in leash or let them go. But in falconry, no beginner can hunt so easily, either by carrying his birds, or by setting them at their prey. Falcons and other hawks become clumsy or impossible to manage, if they are handled badly. The most ignorant of men may learn something about other kinds of hunting, just by using their ears and eyes, but without a teacher of experience, and without constant practice under expert guidance, no one, noble or commoner, can obtain even an elementary knowledge of falconry.
>
> It can be claimed that, since many nobles and but few commoners learn and conscientiously follow this art, that it is, by its nature, a sport of the aristocracy. Further, one can say

CHAPTER 9. JOUSTING & HUNTING

that it is nobler, more worthy and superior to all other kinds of hunting. [*The Art of Hunting with Birds*]

Frederick gives a detailed description of the long and complicated training of falcons. The following is just one stage in the process. It came after the bird had been "seeled," that is, had its eyelids sewn together so that it was blind. The stitches were, of course, removed in due time:

> 95. After the seeled falcon has been placed on the wrist, she should stay there for some time, and gently carried round in a dark room, alone with her keeper. This must go on for a day and a night. If possible, she should not even be allowed to rest on a perch or a block. So that this can be done without too much discomfort she may be moved from hand to hand and men may take turns to carry her. What is more, during all this time, she should not be fed, so that on the second day she is very hungry.
>
> The falconer should now have a chicken leg in his pouch, and should take the bird into the dark, quiet room where she will be more easily persuaded to eat this food for the first time. This precaution may seem unnecessary, for the bird is seeled, but her thin eyelids do not keep out the light and she will be reluctant to eat, since the daylight reminds her of her life in the wild. It is also important for the room to be quiet, so that the bird is not disturbed by the voices of men, the barking of dogs or other sounds unfamiliar to her.
>
> The falcon is taught to eat in the following way. The meat is held before her, so that she can smell it. Then the falconer touches her beak, breast and feet with it. This is done to irritate the bird, so that she will snap at the meat. Then, when she bites it, the taste will please her and she will eat some or all of it, especially if she is hungry. She will then be so keen to feed that unusual noises will not distract her. Now is the time for the falconer to make a soothing sound, to encourage her to feed. A line from a song will do, so that, in future, it will remind her of food, and whenever she hears

it, she will expect to be fed. The nature of the sound does not matter, but it must always be the same.

At first, the falcon should not be given the whole of the chicken leg. Instead, some should be kept and given to her in small pieces through the day, and always accompanied by the same sound. In that way, the bird will soon become attached to her keeper, grow accustomed to taking food from him, and not be disturbed by his presence. [Ibid.]

Later stages involved training the unseeled falcon to fly to a lure, flung on the ground, and to "stoop" on a live bird released in front of her. With a peregrine that was to hunt ducks, the final stage was to learn "waiting on." That meant circling above the falconer until beaters frightened the ducks into flight, whereupon the peregrine stooped on one of them. Much could go wrong:

96. When the falcon leaves her falconer to visit another man she has seen, the falconer can follow her quite easily. She is hoping that the first man will fling a lure, or put up some bird for her to capture. She is not going far and does not tire herself. When she reaches the man, she will wait on above him, hoping he will throw her the lure. But since he does not call to her, throw the lure or do anything to attract her, she will soon realize her mistake and return to her falconer. He is the one that calls to her and waves his glove.

Sometimes a falcon ceases to wait on just because she wants to go and perch. It is more serious if there is no obvious reason for this, or if she does it just because she has found a good place to rest.

A falcon may leave her falconer because she is frightened by another bird, especially if she is timid by nature, or a beginner. A young falcon is easily put off by the arrival of hostile birds. Certain birds threaten to mob her, so that she sometimes perches, and sometimes flies so far away that the falconer finds it difficult to entice her back. The further she flies, the worse it is, for even though she may return she will be too tired to hunt. More than that, she may go so far astray that she is lost. [Ibid.]

There were several kinds of falcons and numerous kinds of prey, and each type of hunting brought its own thrills and its own problems. It is easy to understand the appeal that the sport had for an intelligent man, since there were endless skills and an immense amount of knowledge to be mastered.

HUNTING

Hunting with dogs, especially on horseback, brought a different kind of excitement, that of physical danger to the huntsman. Like jousting, it was seen as a preparation for war. The following description of a hunt is taken from the anonymous epic about Siegfried that inspired Wagner:

97. Brave Siegfried slew whatever animal the hounds started. His horse ran so fast that none escaped him. With his own hands, he killed the first animal of the hunt, a strong young boar. Soon afterwards, be found a huge lion [poetic license here]. He shot it with his bow, after which the lion made only three more leaps. Siegfried's companions applauded. Then, in rapid succession, he slew a bison, an elk, four aurochs and a giant deer. He rode so swiftly that neither hart nor hind could escape him. Then the hound started an enormous boar. It tried to flee, but Siegfried barred its way. The boar charged him ferociously, but he killed it with his sword, a feat which almost any other hunter would have found impossible.

Then the huntsmen said, "Lord Siegfried, leave something for us to kill. You will empty both our mountain and our forest of game." [*The Nibelungenlied*]

Like falconry, hunting had its enthusiastic addicts. It was praised by Edward, duke of York, in his book, *The Master of the Game*. York was cousin to both Richard II and Henry IV. He wrote his book when in prison, accused of plotting to assassinate Henry, and, perhaps, hoping to win favor, he dedicated his work to the king's son, the future Henry V. York was released from prison, only to die in the English vanguard at the Battle of Agincourt:

98. To the honor and reverence of you, my right worshipful and dread lord, Henry, by the grace of God, son and heir unto the high, excellent and Christian Prince, Henry IV, by the aforesaid grace, King of England and France, Prince of Wales, Duke of Guienne, of Cornwall and Earl of Chester.

I, your own in all humility, have ventured to make this simple book, which I recommend and submit to your noble and wise correction, which book, if it pleases your Lordship, shall be called Master of the Game. And for this cause that this book treats of what in every season of the year is most lasting, and to my thinking to every gentle heart most enjoyable of games, that is to say, hunting. For though hawking with gentle hounds and hawks for the heron and water fowl be noble and commendable, it seldom lasts at most for half the year. For though men find from May to Lammas game enough to hawk at, no one will find hawks to hawk with. But as to hunting, there is no season of all the year in which game may not be found in every good country, also hounds ready to chase it.

Now I shall prove how hunters live in this world more joyfully than any other men. For when the hunter rises in the morning, and sees a sweet and fair morn and clear, bright weather, and hears the song of small birds, which sing so sweetly with great melody and full of love, each in its own language in the best way it can; and when the sun is up and he sees fresh dew upon the small twigs and grasses, and the sun by his power makes them shine, that is great

joy and plea-
sure to the
hunter's heart.

And when
he shall go to
his quest or
searching, he
shall see or
soon meet
with the hart
without great
seeking and
shall trace him

to his lair. It is a great joy and pleasure to the hunter.

When the hounds have passed before him, then shall he ride
after them and shout and blow as loudly as he can, with great joy
and pleasure, and I assure you he thinks of no sin or other evil
thing.

When the hart is overcome and at bay, he shall be glad. And
later, when the hart is dead, he cuts him up and rewards his hounds,
and so he shall have great pleasure; and when he comes home, he
comes joyfully.

And when he has come home he shall doff his clothes and shall
wash his legs, and perhaps all his body. In the meanwhile he shall
order his supper, of vegetables and the neck of the hart and other
good wine and ale. And when he has eaten and drunk, he shall be
glad and well at his ease. Then he shall go and drink and lie in his
bed in fresh clothes, and shall sleep soundly all night, without any
thoughts of sin. Therefore I say that hunters go into Paradise when
they die, and live in this world more joyfully than other men. [*The
Master of the Game*, c. 1410]

Thomas of Chantimpré, a Dominican friar from Brabant, held other
views on the ultimate destination of hunters:

99. There is a kind of game, of those who sport with the
fowls of the air and the hounds of the earth; whereof the

damnation is most manifest in clerics, who wander about after such sports and neglect their due service to Christ. Yet even in noble laymen those things may be seen to be damnable, if, on this account, they neglect and despise their daily prayers and masses.

A certain knight of high degree was wont to compel many of his tenants daily to wander and spend their labor in hunting with him; whereby very many left their own business of tilling the fields, and fell with their wives and children into poverty and want. It befell therefore one day that he went into the forest to chase the stag with his own servants and his household and the hounds were in full cry, and he followed the game with all his might on horseback. But when he had ridden all day in vain, and still saw the stag fleeing ever before his face, then his mind was turned to madness, and pursued after him all night long with his whole train so that day forward no man ever saw or knew what had become of them, or whither they were gone. Some said (and we easily believe it) that the earth opened her jaws to swallow them up and sucked them down to hell. [*Bonum Universale de Apibus,* c. 1260]

THE JUDICIAL DUEL

The judicial duel was a legal procedure, intended to prove guilt or innocence. The accused defended himself against his accuser in a combat, the idea being that God would side with the party who was in the right and grant him victory. Such a fight was certainly not a pastime for the protagonists, though it was likely to be entertaining for the spectators.

Once very common, the combat became more and more unpopular, because it seemed that God was nearly always on the side of the strong. We have seen [reading 57] how the procedure was abused in the reign of Richard ɪɪ of England, with lusty young men making false accusations against others who were old and frail. One answer was to employ champions, but that favored the wealthier of the litigants, since he could hire the better man.

CHAPTER 9. JOUSTING & HUNTING

The Emperor Frederick II had misgivings about the combat and he forbade it almost completely by his *Constitutions of Melfi*. He retained it only for cases of treason, murder by secret means and poisoning, hoping that the thought of a combat would deter people who were contemplating any of these crimes. A judge could also allow a combat, if no other means of proof was available. Frederick did, though, make rules to ensure that the combat would be as fair as possible:

100. TITLE XXXVII. HOW CHAMPIONS MUST FIGHT
We order that champions must have clubs that are exactly the same, without thorns, horns, knobs or hooks.

TITLE XXXVIII. WHAT OATH MUST BE SWORN BY CHAMPIONS
Champions must take oaths as soon as they enter the ring. They must swear that they believe the lords they represent are telling the truth and are not guilty of any lies or deceit. They must also swear that they will fight with all their strength, zeal and energy. They must not promise each other that they will avoid damaging hands or teeth, or refrain from inflicting any other kind of injury. Instead, they should try to defeat each other by whatever means they may.

TITLE XXXIX. DECEIT AND TRICKERY BY CHAMPIONS
We must provide a remedy against fraud by champions who are either lazy or afraid of being hurt. If it seems to the referee that a champion is not fighting properly, or is being lazy, or if it appears that he did not do his best to defend himself and was too quick to declare himself the loser, and if the accused would die as a result of his champion being defeated, then the champion himself should suffer death. But if he is fighting for a plaintiff who wishes to assuage sorrow caused by the death of a parent or a close relation, the champion should not be condemned to death, if he is defeated, since he only fought to help those who were sorrowing and to prove the case. In a case of perjury, the champion should only lose his hand, which is the usual punishment for that crime. It is wrong to condemn a champion to

death, when the life of his client was in no danger from the law. However, in cases of treason, the accuser must die, if he fails, just as the defendant would have done, had he lost.

TITLE XL. ON THE STATUS AND AGE OF COMBATANTS

Anyone who offers combat must fight in a way suited to the rank of the defendant, and not in a way chosen by himself. The accused, who is brought to law to defend himself, must not lose the right to choose his own means of defense against another, who might well have concocted a malicious plan to choose a method of fighting that would confuse his opponent, even before the combat began. If a knight is challenged to a combat, and wishes to fight on horseback, his opponent must do the same, even though he is not a knight. But if the defendant is a foot soldier, he should be allowed to fight in his own way, even though his accuser is a knight. So that anyone who has been injured should not suffer in his defense as a result, we order that the challenger should simulate that same injury. If the accused has only one eye, then the challenger must cover his own eye for some days before the combat, and the same principle should apply to the loss of fingers or other limbs. As a further act of kindness we decree that no one over the age of sixty, or under the age of twenty-one, should be made to fight for himself, but may employ a champion. We cannot subject such people to the combat, for whom it is not only uncertain, but dangerous. [*Constitutions of Melfi*]

CHAPTER 10
RELATIONS BETWEEN THE SEXES

MARRIAGE

The medieval church had rules to govern sex and marriage. It encouraged married love, though of a certain kind. The wife, as the subordinate, was expected to honor and obey her husband; the husband was expected to protect and cherish his wife. The love, though, must not be sexual. The church did expect couples to beget children, for there were vacancies to fill in paradise, following the expulsion of Satan and his hordes. Sex simply for pleasure, though, was not allowed and even pleasure in sex was suspect. "The husband who loves his wife too ardently," said St. Jerome, "is guilty of adultery." The ideal married couple made occasional, furtive, and brief descents into iniquity, until they had produced offspring, after which they lived in chastity.

The highest state of all was virginity, a thought which must have comforted many an impotent male, for, like St. Paul, he had "the gift of continence." Next, came marriage, with sexual abstinence, followed by sex within marriage, sex between unmarried couples, adultery by men and, the ultimate horror, adultery by women.

The view of the laity was different. Love might or might not blossom after marriage, but at the time it was of no account. The union could be made to reinforce a political alliance or to amalgamate territories; and nearly always it had the object of producing male heirs.

Seeing a marriage had such serious objectives, it needed to be deliberated with great care, many opinions being sought. Usually, there was only one person of note whose views were not worth having. The Barnwell chronicler describes a royal wedding that took place in 1235:

101. In February of that year, two Templars came to Westminster, accompanied by knights and other solemn messengers. They were sent by Emperor Frederick II to the king of England, and bore letters from him sealed with gold, in which he requested the hand of King Henry III's sister, Isabella, in marriage.

The king of England was very interested in this idea and discussed it for three days with the nobles and bishops of the kingdom. Having carefully weighed the matter, they declared unanimously that Isabella should be given to the emperor, and thus on 27 February, they reported their conclusion and consent to the marriage.

When the envoys asked to see Isabella, the king sent faithful deputies to the Tower of London where his sister lived, carefully protected. They were to bring her into the royal presence and show her to the messengers of the emperor, a beautiful girl in her twenty-first year, distinguished by her maidenhood and bedecked with the usual trappings of royalty.

The ambassadors were pleased with the girl and judged her fitting in every way to be an imperial bride. They offered her a betrothal ring on the emperor's behalf, and when they had placed it on her finger, they shouted together, "Long live the empress!" Then, after the delegates had informed the emperor of their deeds, Frederick II sent the archbishop of Cologne and the duke of Louvain to England with an escort of high-ranking nobles, who were to accompany the empress to him with all honor for the consummation of the marriage.

The preparations for the wedding were so lavish that they seemed to exceed all the riches of the kingdom. For the sake of the empress's dignity, her crown was most skillfully crafted from the purest gold and studded with precious stones. On it were sculpted the four kings of England who were confessors and martyrs, and to whom King Henry had especially commended the care of his sister's soul.

In her festal robes, which were of silk and wool, and also of linen of different hues, decked out in all the dignity that befits an empress, Isabella shone so that it was impossible to tell which of her many adornments would most induce love in the emperor's heart.

In addition to all this, her bed, with its silk covers and brightly colored mattresses, different hangings and draperies sewn from the most delicate muslin, stood so splendidly that its softness actively invited those seeking repose to sweet sleep. All the vessels sent, whether for wine or for food, were cast in completely unalloyed silver and gold, and, what seemed almost superfluous to everyone, even the cooking pots, large and small, were of the finest silver.

The king had procured for his sister a host of well-bred horses of docile temperament which were most distinctive with their coats of different shades and appropriate for the empress's honor, because they would carry their riders gently, without stumbling. They were harnessed in fine tackle, their saddles gilded and wonderfully crafted, with gilded reins and ornamental breastplates, so that the steeds were as splendid as their knights.

The empress and the archbishop of Cologne, with the nobles and ladies-in-waiting assigned to her service, embarked on 11 May, the sails of their huge ships unfurled, and they entrusted themselves to the open sea. There were no tears wanting when the king parted from the empress, a brother from a sister.

At the time of the empress's arrival at Cologne, the emperor was on a military expedition against his rebellious son. Having defeated and thrown his son into chains, Frederick II finally sent for her, bidding her to come to him at Worms. Here, the emperor received her with great rejoicing and honor, because he was delighted by what he saw of the girl whom nature had adorned with a particular glow.

On Sunday, 30 July, Frederick solemnly wed Isabella, the sister of the king of England. Much as she pleased him in outward appearance, she pleased him even more in the marriage bed, when he found signs of her virginal purity. [*The Barnwell Chronicle*]

Frederick was twice the age of his bride and far from handsome. It was said of him, "As a slave in the market he would not have fetched 200 dirhams; and he was red-faced, going bald, had weak eyes."

A year after his sister's marriage, Henry III acquired a wife in much the same way. He sent envoys to Count Raymond of Provence, requesting the hand of his daughter, Eleanor, a girl of twelve. The process resembles mail order, and if the goods were unsatisfactory, excuses could be found for returning them. Jean de Marmoutier relates of Fulk of Anjou:

> 102. Fulk had several wives. There was the daughter of Lancelin of Beaugency, and when she died, Fulk married Ermengardine, daughter of Archenbaud the Strong of Bourbon. She bore him Geoffrey Martel II. The lecherous Fulk then fell madly in love with the sister of Aumary de Montfort, "whom no good man ever praised, except for her beauty." To have her, he put aside Ermengardine, saying that she was related to him. [*Chronicles of the Counts of Anjou*]

Fulk's excuse for disposing of Ermengardine was a common one. The church did not allow divorce, but it also forbade marriage within

no less than seven degrees. If a man tired of his wife, he would instruct clerics to hunt through the genealogies, and it was almost certain that some remote, common ancestor could be found. The man would then declare that he had discovered, to his horror, that he had been guilty of incest. His marriage, therefore, had been invalid and he was free to find another wife. As like as not, his new bride would be more closely related to him than the old one.

It was, of course, possible to find love within marriage. The following poem was written by Christine de Pisan (c. 1363- c. 1431). She was married at fifteen, had several children and was widowed at twenty-five. She then supported herself and her children by her writing, a unique achievement by a woman in those days:

103. A sweet thing is marriage;
I can prove it from my own experience.
It's true for a woman who has a husband
As wise and good as the one God found for me.
Let him be praised who has willingly
Protected me, for I feel
The great worth of his conduct.
And surely my sweet one loves me very much.

The first night of our marriage
I could straightaway appreciate
His great worth, for he never treated me presumptuously,
Or did anything to make me unhappy.
But as soon as it was time to rise,
He kissed me a hundred times, giving me pleasure,
Demanding nothing rude of me.
And surely my sweet one loves me very much.
And he said in such gentle words,
"God permitted me to come to you,
Sweet friend, and in order to serve you
I think he allowed me to prosper."
That is how he ended his reverie
Throughout the night, and that is how he comported
   himself
Steadfastly, never changing his mind.
And surely my sweet one loves me very much.

Prince, loving makes me lose my senses
When he tells me his is wholly mine;

And I'm bursting with sweetness –
And surely my sweet one loves me very much.
[*Aultres Balades*]

ADULTERY

The happiness of Fulk of Anjou, described on a previous page, lasted barely two years. Jean de Marmoutier relates:

> 104. The lascivious King Philip arrived at Tours, and, when he had met Fulk's wife, he decided she would be his queen. That wicked woman left the count the very next night and followed the king. To prevent pursuit, he had placed knights on the bridge over the Beuvron, and he took her to Orléans. And so the lustful king wallowed in adultery, even though he was under sentence of excommunication, and had two sons by the woman. [*Chronicles of the Counts of Anjou*]

There were other interesting situations. Gerald of Wales wrote:

> 105. Count Geoffrey of Anjou, when he was seneschal of France, took advantage of Queen Eleanor; for which reason he often warned his son Henry, telling him above all not to touch her, both because she was his lord's wife, and because he had known her himself. As the final culmination of these outrages it is related that King Henry presumed to sleep adulterously with the said queen of France, taking her from his own lord and marrying her himself. How could anything fortunate, I ask, emerge from these copulations? [*Itinerary through Wales*, c. 1200]

One of the most famous royal affairs was that between Henry II of England, the same Henry who is mentioned above, and Rosamund Clifford. An anonymous ballad tells the story of Rosamund:

> 106. When as King Henry ruled this land,
> The second of that name,
> Besides the queen he dearly loved
> A fair and comely dame.

Most peerless was her beauty found,
Her favor and her face;
A sweeter creature in this world
Could never prince embrace.
Her crisped locks like threads of gold
Appeared to each man's sight;
Her sparkling eyes like Orient pearls,
Did cast a heavenly light.

Yea Rosamund, fair Rosamund,
Her name was called so,
To whom our queen, dame Eleanor,
Was known a deadly foe.

The king therefore, for her defense
Against the furious queen,
At Woodstock builded such a bower,
The like was never seen.

Most curiously that bower was built
Of stone and timber strong,
An hundred and fifty doors
Did to this bower belong.

And they so cunningly contrived,
With turnings round about,
That none but with a clue of thread
Could enter in or out.
[*Ballad of Fair Rosamund*]

It was said that Queen Eleanor found Rosamund in her bower by following a silken thread through the labyrinth. She then stabbed her as she lay in her bath and held her down while she bled to death.

Whatever his own morals were like, the rage of a husband who caught his wife in adultery was dreadful:

107. Philip, count of Flanders, caught Walter of Fontaines in adultery with his wife, Countess Isabel. He had him

clubbed to death and had his body hung upside down on a
lavatory seat, with its feet tied together. And so that no cruelty should be missing and his rage against the dead man
complete, he ordered him to be publicly exposed to the gaze
of all. [Ralph of Diceto, *Images of History*]

[Note: Lavatories in a medieval castle discharged down a long
chute into the moat.]

The writer does not tell us the fate of the countess.

MISOGYNY

Medieval men were ambivalent in their view of women, for Eve
was responsible for the fatal temptation of Adam, while Mary was
the mother of Christ. Usually, the dilemma was resolved by seeing
Mary as absolutely unique and women in general as daughters of
Eve. Here is a priest's view of them:

108. Nor is it wonderful, if a woman follows her innate bad
disposition, for it is written in Ecclesiastes [8:28], "I have
found one good man out of a thousand, but not one good
woman"; and in Ecclesiasticus [25:15-16], "There is no head
above the head of a serpent and there is no wrath above the
wrath of a woman;" and again [cf. 42:14], "Small is the wickedness of man compared to the wickedness of woman."
[Gerald of Wales, *Itinerary Through Wales*, c. 1200]

An anonymous French author wrote:

109. What shall we say of the ladies when they come to feasts?
Each marks well the others' heads. They wear bosses like
horned beasts, and if any have no horns, she is a laughing
stock for the rest. Their arms go merrily when they come
into the room; they display their kerchiefs of silk and cam-
bric, set on their buttons of amber, and cease not to babble
so long as they are in the bower. When they sit down to
dine, they put aside their wimples to open their mouths. If
a squire should enter at that moment, they are sure to mock

him in secret. Two nimble valets have their hands full with serving all these ladies, each to her own fancy. The one is busy fetching their meats from the kitchen and the other drawing good wine from the buttery. When they have eaten at leisure, then they herd together to babble in secret. One tickles the other's heart, if by chance she may entice some secret from it. Then, when dinner hour is come, they descend the steps and trip daintily into the hall, hand in hand. But when they are set down to meat, they touch no morsel of all that is spread before them; right coyly they sit there and show their faces; she whom men most gaze upon is she who bears away the prize. When therefore they have shown all that is in front, they then find some occasion to sweep the bench-backs, that men may see the costly workmanship on their backs, which was hidden in front. [*Ici commencent les actions de dames*, 13th century]

COURTLY LOVE

During the early Middle Ages, young men in search of sexual adventure resorted to the direct, uncomplicated procedure of abduction, hunting indiscriminately unmarried women, wives, widows and nuns. During the later Middle Ages, abduction was replaced by courtly love, which had the same object, but pursued it by an elegant process of seduction. Many a woman welcomed the change. She was no longer the unwilling victim of male lust; she was no longer a pawn in some political or dynastic game; she was no longer the object of misogynist derision. Moreover, instead of lying at the feet of a chauvinistic male, she found herself on a pedestal, with the man prostrate before her.

Christine de Pisan describes a passage of courtly love. The lady does appear to succumb rather easily!

110. She: I'll sell you a hollyhock,

He: Lovely one, I don't dare tell you
How much love draws me to you.

You can see it all without my saying it!
I'll sell you a trembling leaf.

She: Many false lovers put up a front
To make their huge lies seem true.
One shouldn't believe everything they say.
I'll sell you the paternoster.

He: You know very well I'm yours;
I never belonged to anyone else,
So don't refuse me,
Beautiful girl that I love, but without delay
Grant me your love!
I'll sell you a parrot.

She: You're fine and good and gallant,
Sir, and well-bred in every way.
But I've never learned to love,
And I still wouldn't want to learn
How to fall in love or be made love to!

He: I'll sell you a turtle dove.

She: Left all alone and by herself –
Led astray by a man who's fled –
That's how I'd live.

I'd never feel any joy in that,
No matter what I had.

He: I'll sell you a pair of wool gloves.

She: It would be too vile of me
To refuse your love;
Since my love would willingly – if I dared –
Be given to you;
I'd be loved by you,
For you're worthy of having
Helen, and even her lovely person.
I'll sell you a dream of love
That brings either joy or sorrow
To those who've dreamed it.

He: My lady, the dream I've dreamed
All night would come true
If I could win your love.
I'll sell you the soaring lark.

She: Your charming speech
And your fine and gentle manner,
Gentle friend, make my heart joyful,
And so I can't refuse you –
I'll be yours without a quarrel!
[*Je vous vens la passerose: Jeux à vendre*]

The following gives the ideal picture of courtly love:

III. I ask you, castle of Love,
What is your main foundation?
To love loyally.

Now tell me of your great wall,
What makes it so handsome, strong and sure?
To conceal discreetly.

Tell me, what are the battlements,
The windows and the stones?
Adoring looks.

Friends, name me the guardian.
Evil speaking danger.

What key can unlock it?
To beg politely.
[Anon., *Le Chastel d'Amours,* 14th century]

The following extract was written by Walther von der Vogelweide, an Austrian nobleman who became a wandering minstrel, an unlikely occupation for one of knightly stock:

112. On a May morning at dawn, when the blossoms spangle the grass like joyful faces in the merry sunshine, and little birds sing the sweetest tunes they can find in their hearts, what happiness can be compared to this? It is half the kingdom of heaven! Shall I say what it is like? Then shall I tell what has often brought still more happiness to my eyes, and would bring it again, if I could but see it. When a noble lady, fair and clean, daintily clad, goes for pleasure among a crowd of folk, in courtly pride and with a courtly train, looking around her now and again, even as the sun is to the stars, then let May bring her best marvels. What has she that is so enchanting as this lady's lovely shape, to gaze at whom we would turn our backs on all the flowers of spring? [*So die bloumen uz dem grase dringent,* c. 1210]

Charles d'Orléans, a French nobleman of the fifteenth century, lamented the death of his lover in lines worthy of Lamartine:

113. I have said farewell to my lady
Within the chapel of love,
And the mass for her soul
Was sung by doleful thoughts.
Full many candles of piteous sighs
Gave light.
Also, I had the tomb made
Of sorrows.
[*Poems*]

CHAPTER 11
THE HOUSEHOLD

ADMINISTRATION

Dame Alice de Bryene was a lady of gentle birth. In 1386, her husband died and she retired to her manor house at Acton, in the county of Suffolk. The following extracts are from her steward's accounts for 1412-1414. The steward was the most important of the manorial officials, being responsible both for the estate and the household:

114. Tuesday 4 October
Meals: Breakfast 8, dinner 20, supper 20. Sum 48.
The Lady took her meals with the household; in addition, Saltwell with two fellows, Robert Mose, John Teyler with one of his household, and Colbrook for the whole day.
Pantry: 50 white [wheat] loaves and six black [rye?] loaves; wine from what remained; ale from stock.
Kitchen: one quarter of bacon, one joint of mutton, one lamb, 24 pigeons.
Purchases: nil.
Provender: hay from stock for 6 horses; fodder for the same, one bushel of oats. Sum of the purchases, nil.

[Note: Robert Mose was the estate's blacksmith and John Colbrook was the harvester.]

Sunday 25 December. Nativity of the Lord.
The baking: one quarter of wheat, whence came 230 white and 30 black loaves.
Meals: Breakfast 12, dinner 28, supper 20, Sum 60.
Guests: Richard Scrivener, one harper, the whole day, the bailiff of the manor with the harvest reeve and 16 of the

household of the manor, Agnes White, one of the household of Ralph Chamberleyn, one repast.

Pantry: 64 white and 8 black loaves, whereof newly-baked
10 white and 2 black loaves; wine from what remained; ale
from stock.

Kitchen: one quarter of beef, one quarter of bacon, one
young pig, one capon, one cony.

Purchases: beef and pork 2s-8d, veal 3s-od, one young pig
6d, eggs 12d, milk 1½d.

Provender: hay from stock for 7 horses; fodder for the same,
one bushel oats.

Sum of purchases, 7s-3½d.

Sunday 1 January.

The baking: one quarter wheat, whence came 232 white and
36 black loaves.

The brewing: 2 quarters malt, whereof one quarter drage,
whence came 112 gallons of ale.

Meals: Breakfast 30, dinner one hundred 60, supper 30.

Sum, two hundred 40.

William Sampson and his wife and one of his household,
Edward Peyton with one of his household, the wife of Robert Dynham with her son, John Teyler with his son, Richard
Scrivener the bailiff of the manor with the harvest reeve
and 8 of the household of the manor, Margaret Brydbek,
one harper, Agnes Whyte the whole day, Agnes Rokewode
with 2 sons, a daughter and a maidservant, the vicar of
Aketon [Acton] with one of his household, Richard Appylton
with his wife and one of his household, Thomas Malcher
with 300 tenants and other strangers, one repast.

Pantry: 314 white and 40 black loaves, whereof newly baked
104 white and 14 black loaves; wine from what remained; ale
from stock.

Kitchen: 2 pigs, 2 swans, 12 geese, 2 joints of mutton, 24
capons, 17 conies.

Purchases: beef 8s-2d, veal 3s-od, 5 young pigs 2s-4d, 12 gallons of milk 18d.

Provender: hay from stock for 18 horses; fodder for the same,
2 bushels of oats.
Sum of the purchases, 15s-0d.

Thursday, 17 August.
The brewing: 2 quarters malt, whereof one quarter drage,
whence came 112 gallons of ale.
Meals: Breakfast 46, dinner 60, supper 60. Sum 146.
Thomas Malcher, the bailiff of the manor with the harvest
reeve and 16 of the household of the manor, John Scoyl with
40 boon workers, Richard Barbour the whole day.
Pantry: 50 white, and 6 black loaves and 20 loaves for the
boon workers; wine from supply; ale from stock.
Kitchen 1½ quarters of beef, 3 quarters of bacon, 2 joints of
mutton, one lamb, 30 pigeons.
Purchases: milk 4d.
Provender: hay from stock for 7 horses; fodder for the same,
one bushel of oats.
Sum of the purchases, 4d.

Though it is impossible to relate the numbers of meals to the
numbers of people, the arithmetic is correct, save for the total of
meals in the last entry. "Hundred" in letters means the "long hundred," or 120. When the steward meant 100, as we understand it,
he used figures. In the entry for 17 August, he must have meant
"one hundred and 46."

On the vigil of St Michael, that is, 28 September, the steward
summarized his accounts for the year. The following are the expenses for wine and wheat, though most of the wheat used by the
household was grown on its own manor:

115. In one pipe of red wine bought at London by the Lady,
with the expenses for the same and carriage to Colchester,
67s-2d.

Item in 2 pipes and one hogshead of red wine bought of
John Joye of Ipswich by the Lady, £8-13s-4d.

Item in one hogshead of white wine bought of the same, 40s.

Item in one quart of white wine bought there for the Lady, 2d by the Lady.

In expenses of John Pellycan, William Boteler and 2 carters from time to time buying and seeking the said wine at Ipswich, as more fully appears in a certain paper of the Lady, 5s-5d.

In 2 small barrels, whereof one of Rumneye and the other of Malmesyn bought by the Lady at London of William Caundyssh, 36s. Item in expenses for the said 2 barrels of wine, as appears in the said paper of the Lady, 5s-5d. In 12 quarters of wheat bought by the lady of the Rector of Stanstede £4-8s, price 7s-4d the quarter.

Sum, £20-15s-6d.

These are some of the "petty necessaries":

116. Paid to Thomas Mellere, 27 October, for sharpening and setting millstones in the bakehouse of the household for 2½ days, 7½d.

Paid to William Soupere with his mate, 24 November, as for one man for 15 days cutting down timber and making hoops of wood therefrom and repairing vessels in divers offices of the Lady's household, 3s-9d.

Paid to the same William for a new hoop for the great leaden cistern in the bakehouse, 2s, whereof 100 nails for the same hoop, 4d.

Paid to John Tylere and his son one day 3 November, laying tiles in the manor, 5d.

Paid to the same John for one day, 2 January, for mending the great oven in the bakehouse, 4d.

Paid to John Longe, smith, for one lock with one key and one iron latch for the door of the woodyard, 8d.

Paid to the same John Longe for 300 door nails, a hundred 60 great nails for the door of the grange, a hundred 60 window nails, 8 hinges with 8 iron hooks, one latch, one snach, and for nails bought from him at divers times and the mending of rakes, 5s-5d.

Item for 32 cups bought against the feast of the Nativity of Our Lord, 2s-0d.

Paid to John Crab, carpenter, 4 December, hired for 17½ days taking 3d a day, with food, in the household and for one day 5d, without food, with the wage of Robert his son for 14 days taking 2d a day, with food, and one day without food taking 4d, for stacking timber and making anew the door of the barn, and for other necessaries within the manor of Aketon, 7s-5½d.

In expenses of Richard Mody and William Kendale from time to time to take conies against the feast of the Nativity of Our Lord, 20d.

Item paid to John Webbe of Sudbury for 3 quarters 4 bushels of quicklime bought from him for the repair of the house of the manor of Aketon, 4s-4½d.

Item paid to 2 sawyers of Sudbury, 18 April, for sawing one thousand two hundred and 70 foot-boards, 12s-7d, for each hundred 12d by the piece.

Item paid for the remaking and mending of one saddle called "le Samersadel," 5d.

John Hethe, smith, in full payment for shoeing the Lady's horses by the year, viz., for 58 horseshoes price 2d each, for 14 horseshoes price ½d each and for 110 tips price ½d each, 16s-0d.

The following were some of the "kitchen necessaries":

117. In six yards of linen cloth for cleaning the windows and vessels of the kitchen, 20d.

In one "streynour," 2d.

In mending one tripod and one iron cobet in which the spit turns in roasting food, 11d.

In four earthen pans bought to catch the dripping, 6d.

In one pestle for crushing food, 2d.

In one new "dressyngknyf," 20d.

In 2 iron pans for taking the clarified fat, 40d.

It is interesting to compare the prices of the goods with the men's wages in the previous entry.

The following are about servants:

118. In the wages of the Lady's maid and of the chamberlain, squires, chaplains, grooms, clerks of the chapel and boys, of which the parcels more fully appear in the Lady's paper, £44 by the year.

For clothing of divers ministers of the Lady as well for the household servants as for divers others of the Lady's counsel, and bailiffs, farmers and other officers retained in the Lady's service against the feast of the Nativity of Our Lord, £23-17s-1½d.

Item for 20 furs of the said livery for gentlemen, 26s-6d, price each fur on average, 15¾d and ½ a farthing, plus ½d on the whole.

Item paid for summer liveries for the said household servants this year, £10-16d.

The steward's grain accounts show 72 quarters of wheat, 102 quarters of barley and 70 quarters of oats. The wheat was for bread and pies, the barley was for malt and the oats were for horse fodder. Other uses for the grain were feeding hens, geese, partridges and swans and for fattening cygnets. There are also these entries:

119. Green peas.

For one quarter one bushel, received of the bailiff of Aketon.

Sum, one quarter one bushel.

And expended in pottage of the lady and her household servants in the said household one quarter one bushel.

And it balances.

Dried peas.

For one quarter 3 bushels received from the bailiff of Aketon for pigeons' food. And for 3 quarters received of the same bailiff for fodder.

Sum, 4 quarters 3 bushels.

Of which baked for bread, one quarter, mixed with oats, 2 quarters. Expended for the pigeons by John Nowers, keeper of the pigeons, one quarter 3 bushels.

Sum as above, and it balances.

Pigeons

And for 1,216 pigeons received from the issues of the dovecote at Aketon.

Sum 1,216.

Pigeons gave fresh meat in the winter, when it was scarce. Also consumed were 40 pigs, 44 sucking pigs, 46 cattle, 97 sheep and numerous poultry, including 8 young herons.

Fish was eaten on Fridays and Saturdays. The accounts mention 2,510 red herrings, 3,060 white herrings, 240 stockfish, that is, dried fish, 105 salt fish, 200 haddock and quantities of salmon, sturgeon and salt eels.

Salting food was the alternative to refrigerating it, and the household used 7 quarters of salt.

Tallow from the dead animals made 525 lbs of "Paris candles." Fifty pounds of wax, which had to be bought, made superior candles for the chapel and Dame Alice's private rooms. Ten pounds of cotton were needed for the wicks.

Finally, this is the list of spices and condiments purchased:

120. In 3 lb pepper bought at London, 6s-3d, price 2s-1d the lb.

Item in one lb pepper bought at Steresbregge, 23d.

In ½ lb of saffron, 7s-6d.

In 2 lb ginger, 3s-10d, price 23d the lb.

In 2 lb cinnamon, 3s-2d, price 19d the lb.

In one lb cloves bought at Steresbregge, 3s-0d.

In one lb mace, 2s-6d.

In 2 lb soda ash, 20d.

In 40 lb almonds, 8s-4d, price 2½d the lb.

In 4 lb rice, 4d.

In 2 bushels one peck seed-mustard, 2s-3d, price 12d a bushel.

In one frail and 4 lb figs, 4s-8d.
In 6 lb dates, 20d, of which 2 lb, price 8d, and 4 lb, price 12d.
In one frail and 2 lb raisins, 4s-3d.
In 8 lb raisins of Corinth 2s-od, price 3d the lb.
In one lb white sugar bought by the said steward, 18d.
Sum, 54s-10d.
Whereof expended by the lady, 53s-4d, by the steward, 18d.
[*The Household Book of Dame Alice de Bryene*]

It was the high cost of spices which encouraged fifteenth-century explorers to look for a sea route to the East Indies, and so led to the accidental discovery of America.

MEALS

Here are the breakfasts of the more important members of the household of the powerful earl of Northumberland:

121. Braikfastis for my lorde and my lady. Furst a Loof of Brede in Trenchors ij Manchetts [small loaves] j Quart of Bere a Quart of Wyne half a Chyne of Muton or ells a Chyne of Beif Boilid.

Braikfastis for my Lorde Percy [Henry, the eldest son, aged 11] and Mr Thomas Percy. Item Half a lo of houshold Breide. A Manchett j Potell [half a gallon] of Bere a Chekynge [chicken] or ells iij Muton Bonys boyled.

Braikfastis for the Nurcy for my Lady Margaret and Mr Yngram Percy. Item a Machet j Quarte of Bere and iij Muton Bonys boiled.

CHAPTER 11. THE HOUSEHOLD

Braikfasts for my Ladys Gentylwomen. Item a loif of Household Breid a Pottell of Beire and iiij Muton Bonys boyled or ells a Pece of Beif Boilid.

Braikfasts for my Lords Breder [brother] his Hede Officers of Household and Counsaill. Item ij Loofs of Houshold Briede and a Manchet a Gallon of Bere ij Muton Bonys and ij Peces of Beif Boilid. [*Northumberland Household Books*, 1512]

The following is an account of the supper:

122. Many things are necessary to honour the supper, and were all in Ahasuerus's feasts, as is written in the first chapter of the Book of Esther.

The first is a suitable time, for it is convenient that a supper be made in due time, not too early, nor too late. The second, is suitable place, large, pleasant and secure. The third is the heart and glad cheer of him that maketh the feast. The supper is not worthy to be praised, if the lord of the house be unhappy [hevy cheryd]. (Esther 1:12, "When he waxeth hot etc."). The fourth is many diverse dishes, so that who that will not of one, may taste of another (Esther 1:8, "There were brought in dish upon dish"). The fifth is diverse wines and drinks (Esther 1:7, "Wine was brought etc."). The sixth is courtesy and honesty of servants. The seventh is kind friendship and company of them that sit at the supper (Esther 1:3, "He made a feast unto all the Medes"). The eighth is mirth of song and of instruments of music. Noble men do not make suppers without harp or symphony (Luke 15:25, "When he heard the symphony and cornemuse etc."). The ninth is plenty of light of candles and of prickets and of torches. For it is a shame to sup in darkness, and perilous also for flies and other filth. Therefore candles and prickets are set on candlesticks and chandeliers, and lanterns and lamps are lit. The tenth is deliciousness of all that is set on the board. For it is not usual at supper to serve large amounts of common food [greate meate and comin], as at dinner, but with special light, delicious food, especially in noble houses. The eleventh is the long lasting of the supper. For food eaten too hastily, causes trouble at night [grevethe ayenste nyghte]. Therefore at supper men should eat at leisure and not too hastily. Therefore Ahasuerus feasted during the space of 150 days. The twelfth is security. For every man shall be invited to the feast without harm or damage. After a supper that is freely given, it is not honest to make a man pay his reckoning. The thirteenth is liking of rest and of sleep. After supper men shall rest, for then sleep is sweet and pleasant. And therefore beds of ivory and gold were spread upon the pavements in Ahasuerus's palace, as is said in Esther [1:6]. For as Constantine says, "When smoke of meat cometh into the brain, men sleep easily." [*Trevisa's Bartholomew*]

Dinner was a morning meal, and supper was eaten in the afternoon. Over the centuries, meals have become later and later until supper has been shunted off the end of the day.

SERVANTS

The court of the dukes of Burgundy was renowned for its elaborate rituals. One of its members, Olivier de la Marche, describes the duties of the pantler:

123. The duke has a chief pantler and fifty esquire assistants, who come under the authority of the chief pantler both in war and peace, and who are controlled by five gentlemen of the bed-chamber appointed by the duke and each one of whom has nine pantlers under him, who all ride under the standard of the chief pantler.

When the duke is about to dine and when his table has been laid, the usher on duty goes to fetch the pantler on duty that day and escorts him to the pantry. And there the butler of the pantry hands him a napkin and kisses it as a sign of service. The pantler places the napkin on his left shoulder, one end hanging in front, the other behind. The butler then hands him the covered salt-cellar which the afore-mentioned pantler has to carry with his fingers, holding the base and center of the dish, unlike the goblet which is held by the stem. And the pantler, bare-headed, follows the usher.

The pantler places the meat on the table, tastes it, then hands it to the others one after the other. Then the pantler takes up his position at the end of the table in front of the dish and gives the duke two helpings, and each time he helps him to twelve or thirteen dishes. The meal is served in one sitting. And the pantler has to take one of the knives

and put salt from the large dish into the small dish, taste it, and place it in front of the duke.

The pantler takes the biscuits from the side-board and if there is an assembly of people at the banquet, he may place the biscuits before all those seated at the duke's table, but not before the others. [*Mémoires sur l'état de la maison du duc*, 15th century]

The most senior of the lord's personal attendants was his chamberlain, who, as the name suggests, was responsible for the chamber, or bedroom. Here is advice for this servant:

124. The duty of a chamberlain is to be diligent in office, neatly clad, his clothes not torn, hands and face well washed and head well kempt.

See that your lord has a clean shirt and hose, a tunic, a doublet and a long coat, if he wear such, his hose well-brushed, his socks at hand, his shoes or slippers as brown as a water-leech.

In the morning, against your lord shall rise, take care that his linen be clean, and warm it at a clear fire, not smoky, if the weather be cold or freezing.

When he rises make ready the foot-sheet, and forget not to place a chair or some other good seat with a cushion on it before the fire, with another cushion for his feet. Over the cushion and chair spread this sheet so as to cover them; and see that you have a kerchief and a comb to comb your lord's head.

Then pray your lord in humble words to come to a good fire and array him thereby, and there to sit or stand pleasantly; and wait with due manners to assist him. First hold out to him his tunic, then his doublet while he puts in his arms, and have his stomacher well-aired to keep off harm as also his stockings and socks.

Then draw on his socks and his hose by the fire, and lace or buckle his shoes, draw his hose on well and truss them to the height that suits him, lace his doublet in every hole, and put around his neck and on his shoulders a kerchief; and then gently comb his head with an ivory comb, and give him water wherewith to wash his hands and face.

Then kneel down on your knee and say thus, "Sir, what robe or gown doth it please you to wear today?" Then get him such as he asks for, and hold it out for him to put on, and put on his girdle, tight or loose, arrange his robe in the proper fashion, give him a hood or hat for his head, a cloak or cape for the house, according as it be fair or foul, or all misty with rain.

Prepare his pew before he goes to church; then return in haste to your lord's chamber, strip the clothes off the feather bed, and beat the feather bed, but not so as to waste any feathers, and see that the blankets and sheets be clean. When you have made the bed properly, cover it with a coverlet, spread out the bench-covers and cushions, set up the head-sheet and pillow and remove the basin. See that the carpets be laid round the bed and dress the windows and the cupboard with tapestries and cushions. See there be a good fire in the chamber, with plenty of wood and fuel.

You must attend busily to your lord's wardrobe, to keep clothes well, and to brush them cleanly. Use a soft brush, and remember that over-much brushing easily wears out cloth.

Never let woollen clothes or furs go a seven-night without being brushed or shaken, for moths are always ready to alight in them and engender; so always keep an eye on drapery and skinnery.

If your lord take a nap after his meal to digest his stomach, have ready a kerchief and comb, pillow and head-sheet; yet be not far from him – take heed what I say – for much sleep is not good in the middle of the day, and have ready water and towel so that he may wash after his sleep.

When he has supped and goes to his chamber, spread forth your foot-sheet, take off his gown or whatever garment he wears, and lay it up in such a place as ye best know. Put a mantle on his back to keep his body from cold, and set him on the foot-sheet, and pull off his shoes, socks, and hose and throw these last over your shoulder, or hold them on your arm. Comb his hair, but first kneel down and put on his kerchief and night cap. Have the bed ready; and when he is in bed, there to sleep, set there his night light with wax or Paris candle, and see that there is enough to last the night; drive out the dog and the cat, giving them a clout, take no leave of your lord, but bow low to him and retire.

If your lord wishes to bathe and wash his body clean, hang sheets round the room, every one full of flowers and sweet green herbs, and have five or six sponges to sit or lean upon, and see that you have one big sponge to sit upon, and a sheet over so that he may bathe there for a while, and have a sponge also for under his feet, if there be any to spare, and always be careful that the door is shut. Have a basin full of hot, fresh herbs and wash his body with a soft sponge, rinse him with fair, warm rose water, and throw it over him; then let him go to bed but see that the bed be sweet and nice; and first put on his socks and slippers that he may go near the fire and stand on his foot-sheet, wipe him dry with a clean cloth and take him to bed to cure his troubles. [*The Babees Book,* 1447]

Nobles used to send their sons to serve as pages in each others' households. This is the story of one such page:

125. When I was still a little child, I often heard wise men say that no man could ever come to any worth his whole life long, unless he was willing, steadfastly, to serve good women. I was then only a child, and so young that I still rode my hobby-horses, but I thought in my simplicity, "Since pure women so exalt a man, I will always serve the ladies with body, goods, spirit and life." In such thoughts I grew until my twelfth year. Then it happened that I heard of a lady who was much praised and in whom men found goodness. She was of high birth, fair, chaste and pure. I remained in this lady's service for nearly five years.

My soul and body were resolved to woo this fair lady, and when I stood before her and looked lovingly on her, I said to myself, "O happiness! Shall this be my own sweet lady? But how can I serve her as she deserves, better than so many other noble boys in her service? It may be that one of them will serve her better, and that my lady will hate me. All I can do is serve her early and late, yet it may be that some other who loves her less may serve her better. Nevertheless, in love at least, I will excel them all."

In summer, I often picked flowers and brought them to my lady, and when she took them in her white hand, I thought with joy, "Where thy hand is now, there has my own hand been." When I saw others pour water on the lily-white hands of my beloved, I would secretly take away this water that she had touched and drink it for love of her. Thus, in my childish way, I served her well, until my father took me from her. That day I knew deep sorrow and the power of love. My body did indeed depart, but my heart remained, for it would not come with me. [Ulrich von Liechtenstein, *Frauendienst*]

Later, Ulrich was knighted and sent some verses to the lady by his aunt, who was to say how much he loved her. The lady's reply was that, even if he were her equal, she could never abide his hare-lip.

THE MAIN ROOM in a conventional manor house was the hall [see plan left and photo facing page 141], which was the full height of the building and open to the roof. It was not unlike a church without aisles, and was about as difficult to heat.

FIDDLEFORD MANOR HOUSE, DORSET. At either end of this hall was a wing, two storeys high. The ground floor was for storage and the upper floor was the solar, or "sun room." Most of the servants lived, worked, ate and slept in the hall, while the solars gave the owner and his family some

privacy. Fiddleford has lost one of its wings and half of its hall. What is left of the hall is to the right. The surviving solar wing is to the viewer's left.

SOLAR OF FIDDLEFORD MANOR HOUSE The fancy roof gives a touch of refinement, and the fireplace [right] a touch of comfort. In the hall, the fire was in the middle of the floor. The window at the far end, now blocked, has a seat where the lady of the house could have done her needlework.

156

CHAPTER 11. THE HOUSEHOLD

TIMBER ROOF, LACOCK, WILTSHIRE This type of roof was typical of both barns and the halls of manor houses. Here, we have an arch-braced collar beam roof. The collar beams are the timbers that run from side to side, joining the rafters. The arch braces are the curved timbers supporting the collar beams.

BRADLEY MANOR HOUSE, NEWTON ABBOT, DEVON, early and late 15th century. The doorway leads to a porch, which in turn opens into the hall. At a later stage, a covered passage was built on the face of the hall to lead to the chapel, on the right.

There is one solar wing to the left of the doorway, with splendid oriel windows. On the ground floor of this wing there are a buttery, or wine store, and the kitchen. The other solar wing, a much smaller one, is behind the chapel.

CHAPTER 12
KNIGHTS AND ARCHERS

WE SAW IN CHAPTER 2 that, in recent years, it has been shown that the "feudal system" was not as well defined as was, perhaps, once imagined. Nonetheless, the traditional model is still a useful guide, as long as it is not accepted as universally valid. Generally speaking, the situation was that vassals held fiefs from their lords and, in return, gave military service. We have also seen that after the adoption of the stirrup, mounted knights dominated war, so that infantry counted for little. Broadly speaking, all this remained true until the fourteenth century, when the English found a new way of raising armies, which superseded the feudal levy. They also employed a new weapon and new tactics, which swung the advantage back to the infantry.

Under the feudal system, a knight was expected to fight in his lord's army, at his own expense, for up to forty days a year, an arrangement that had many disadvantages, not the least being that some vassals were women or minors [see reading 16]. Also, the feudal host was often unreliable, being officered by arrogant nobles striving to outshine their rivals. But in the fourteenth century, English kings realized that they could have more efficient armies if, instead of calling on the feudal levy, they made contracts with their magnates. Such a contract was known as an "indenture." It would state the nobleman's responsibility, for example, to take charge of the war in a particular area, and it would state what forces he must raise to carry out the task. In return, the king agreed to pay the nobleman for his services.

Another way of raising troops was by Commissions of Array. The commissioners, usually experienced soldiers, would visit towns and villages, demand to see all males aged between sixteen and sixty, and then make a selection. They offered pay, which was about the same rate as that of a skilled craftsman, and they offered pardons for criminal offenses. The chief inducement, though, was the hope of plunder. There were plenty of volunteers to fight a war in France, but commissioners usually had to resort to conscription when raising an army for a war in Scotland, where there was little worth taking.

Nobles and knights still formed the elite of the army, but they were forced to modify their armor. Until about 1300 it was made f r o m   chain mail, that is, a multitude of tiny links of steel. This became obsolete with the development of the longbow, an arrow from which might pierce the mail and drive pieces of it into the wound. During the fourteenth century there was, as a result, a gradual transition to plate mail. At first, it protected only the knees and thighs, but it gradually extended until, by the early fifteenth century there were suits of armor containing no chain mail at all. The best of these suits were made in Italy, especially Milan. They were superb works of craftsmanship that gave the wearer excellent protection, while allowing him freedom of movement. Experiments at the New York Metropolitan Museum showed that a man in plate armor could run, jump, and lie on his face or back and get up, all with great ease. Few, though, could afford such armor and remained vulnerable to the archers. Also, it was impossible to protect much more than the head and chest of a horse. For a time, therefore, the longbow was supreme on the field of battle.

It was the Welsh who first developed the longbow as a truly formidable weapon, Gerald of Wales, wrote:

126. The people of South Wales are more accustomed to war, more famous for valor, and more expert in archery, than those of any other part of Wales. The following examples are proof of this. In the capture of a castle, which happened

in our days, two soldiers were passing over a bridge to take refuge in a tower, when the Welsh, taking them in the rear, penetrated with their arrows the oaken door of the tower which was four fingers thick; in memory of which event, the arrows were preserved in the gate. William de Braose also testifies that one of his soldiers, in a conflict with the Welsh, was wounded by an arrow, which passed through his thigh and the armor with which it was cased on both sides, and through the saddle, so that it mortally wounded the horse. Another soldier had his hip, also sheathed in armor, penetrated by an arrow quite to the saddle, and, on turning his horse round, received a similar wound on the opposite hip, which fixed him to both sides of his seat. What more could be expected from a ballista? Yet the bows used by this people are not made of horn, ivory or yew, but of wild elm; unpolished, rude and uncouth, but stout; not calculated to shoot an arrow to a great distance, but to inflict very severe wounds in close fight. [*Itinerary through Wales*]

These are legends, and it is impossible to say how much truth there is in them. In the hands of a good archer, the longbow had a maximum range of nearly 300 yards. It was effective up to about half that distance, when it was capable of piercing chain mail, if not oak doors and plate armor. The crossbow, a more powerful weapon, was effective up to 250 yards, but its rate of fire was only two shots per minute, in which time a well trained longbowman could deliver ten or a dozen aimed shots. Thus a force of 3,000 archers could put down a barrage of more than 30,000 arrows a minute, and no force of cavalry, however well armored, could ride through it.

It was Edward I (1272-1307) who introduced the longbow to England. During his conquest of Wales, his armies suffered so much at the hands of the Welsh that he saw the wisdom of adopting their traditional weapon. The one problem with the longbow was that it took a long time to learn how to use it with any degree of skill, and even then, constant practice was necessary. The English, though, made the longbow their own. Soon, every town and village had its "butts" where the men and youths held endless contests, so that the army was never short of trained archers.

Laws were passed to encourage archery. Froissart wrote that in 1337, "It was decreed that no man should use any play or pastime save only the longbows and arrows, on pain of death; and that every bowyer and fletcher should be made quit of all his debts." This attachment to the longbow persisted long after firearms had made it largely obsolete. As late as 1550, Archbishop Latimer held that its use was not only a patriotic, but a moral duty:

127. There is such dycing houses also, they say, as hath not bene wont to be, where young gentlemen dice away theyr thrift, and, where dycing is, there are other follies also. For the love of God let remedy be had, let us wrastle and stryve agains sinne. Men of England in tymes past, when they would exercise themselves (for we must needes have some recreation, our bodies can not endure without some exercise) they were wont to goe abroad in the fieldes a Shoot-ing, but now it is turned into glossing, gulling, and whooring within the house. The Arte of Shooting hath bene in times past much esteemed in this realme, it is a gift of God that he hath geve us to excell all other nations withall, it hath bene Gods instrument wherby he hath geven us many victories against our enemyes. But now we have taken up whooring in townes, in stead of Shooting in the feeldes. A wondrous thing that so excellent a gift of God should be so little esteemed.

I desire you my Lordes, even as ye love the honour and glory of God, and entend to remove his indignation, let there be sent forth some proclamation, some sharpe proclamation to the Justices of the Peace, for they doe not their duetie. Justices now be no Justices; there be many good actes made for this matter already. Charge them upon their allegiance, that this singular benefite of God may be practiced, and that it be not turned into bolling, glossing, and whooring within the townes; for they be negligent in executing these lawes of Shooting.

In my time, my poore father was as diligent to teach me to Shoote, as to learne me any other thing, and so I thinke other men did their children. He taught me how to draw, how to lay my body in my bowe, and not to draw with strength of armes as other nations doe, but with strength of the body. I had my bowes bought me, according to my age and strength; as I encreased in them so my bowes were made bigger and bigger: for men shall never Shoote well, except they be brought up in it. It is a goodly Arte, a wholesome kinde of exercise, and much commended in Phisicke. [*Sermon before King Edward vi*]

As well as adopting the longbow, the English developed new tactics. They learnt a hard lesson at Bannockburn, in Scotland, in 1314. The Scottish infantry carried pikes eighteen feet long and they were grouped in tight formations known as "schiltroms" so that their weapons formed an impenetrable hedge. The English cavalry made a vigorous, but reckless charge, only to come to grief on the Scottish spears. The English archers, who could have done great damage to the schiltroms, dared not shoot, for fear of hitting their own cavalry in the back.

After Bannockburn, the English decided that if they were to win battles, they must give up some of the sacred principles of chivalry. In the first place, they abandoned the wild, heroic charge against impossible odds and, instead, stood on the defensive, whenever possible. Secondly, they made their men-at-arms fight on foot. This divorce of the knight from his horse must have been hard to bear, for the most noble form of knightly conduct was to fight mounted. But covered in armor as he was, the knight was much less vulnerable without his horse. Further, being on foot meant his chances of indulging in heroics were much less. Finally, the knights had to accept that the humble men in the army, the archers, were the ones who would do most to bring victory.

One of the many battles which showed the worth of the English tactics was Homildon Hill, a battle against the Scots in 1402. The chronicler exaggerates the effect of the arrows on the armor. Most of the damage would have been done to the horses:

128. At that time the Scots, made restless by their usual arrogance, entered England in hostile fashion, for they thought that all the northern lords had been kept in Wales by royal command. But the earl of Northumberland and the Lord Henry Percy, and Henry his son, and the earl of Dunbar who had lately left the Scots and sworn fealty to the king of England, with an armed band and a force of archers, suddenly flung themselves across the path of the Scots, who, after burning and plundering, wanted to return to their own country, so that the Scots had no choice but to stop and choose a place of battle. They chose therefore a hill near the town of Wooler, called Homildon Hill, where they assembled with their men-at-arms and archers. Without delay, our archers, drawn up in the dale, shot arrows at the Scottish schiltrom, to provoke them to come down. In reply, the Scottish archers directed all their fire at our archers; but they felt the weight of our arrows, which fell like a storm of rain, and so they fled. The earl of Douglas, who was the leader of the Scots, saw their flight, and did not want to seem to desert the battle-field; so he seized a lance and rode down the hill with a troop of horse, trusting too much in his equipment and that of his men, who had been improving their armor for three years, and strove to rush on the archers. When the archers saw this, they retreated, but still firing, so vigorously, so resolutely, so effectively, that they pierced the armor, perforated the helmets, pitted the swords, split the lances and pierced all the equipment with ease. The earl of Douglas was pierced with five wounds, notwithstanding his elaborate armor. The rest of the Scots who had not descended the hill turned tail and fled from the flight of arrows. But flight did not avail them, for the archers followed them, so that the Scots were forced to give themselves

up, for fear of the death-dealing arrows. The earl of Douglas was captured; many of those who fled were captured, but many were drowned in the River Tweed, so that the waters devoured, so it was said, 500 men. In this fight, no English lord or knight received a blow from the enemy but God almighty gave the victory miraculously to the English archers alone, and the magnates and men-at-arms remained idle spectators of the battle. [Thomas of Walsingham, *History of England*]

Fighting in much the same way, the English won several important battles against the French and their allies during the Hundred Years War. These included Crécy in 1346, Poitiers in 1356, Nájera in 1367 and Agincourt in 1415. For their part, the French depended for far too long on the feudal levy, which was unreliable and undisciplined. Their knights insisted on charging heroically in the tradition of chivalry, and perished in a hail of arrows.

v ñ werte der iec menge zo
ḣ mz vf die zir de ñ daute
ḣ es̄ mit trefrelicher wer
Y v satze sich d heidine ler
v ke ſyon gein den geſtin
Y ñ begundin weſtin   zoh
Den be mit starch z gewin hoh
Dar in diw heidin schafte ſich
v ñ tribm vmb̄ haft kur vō m
Ḣ z der selbin veste hin
C rumbe hvfthaże blindin
S we ſtv d mohten vmdin

D ie tribuns vñ d veſt dan   Y mlegend ver gemve
D auvr die wm ſtat geivan   v ñ kenel hoch d hol vz trúe
v ñc darinne kur den be   D e wazzir wnd veſte hin
N v hate de werlich wer   O ch haten ſw wege vz vñ in

CHAPTER 13
SIEGES

WE HAVE ALREADY SEEN one very effective siege method: the mines used by Edward the Black Prince to topple the walls of Limoges in 1370 (reading 84). But there were other means. In 1159 the Emperor Frederick I (Barbarossa) laid siege to the Italian city of Crema. The poet who described Barbarossa's campaigns in Italy gave an account of the siege. There is mention of two siege engines. One was a wooden tower, which was made higher than the walls and then wheeled up to them. It had a draw bridge which could be dropped on to the top of the wall, and used for an assault. Should that prove impossible, then the tower was a vantage point from which to bombard the defenders inside the fortress. The other device was the "tortoise," a strong timber shelter which was pushed to the base of a wall and under which men made a breach with the aid of a battering ram, here described as a "column." It will be seen that one of the most effective means of defense was the sortie, but this was only possible for a large garrison:

> 129. Now Crema was surrounded by their legions,
> And a machine for breaking walls was built.
> The roar, the threats, the tumult of the battle,
> These horrid sounds were cutting through the air.
> Yet the youth inside the fort, who held the gates
> And manned the walls with arms, were hardly frightened,
> Though their voices sometimes raged and sometimes threatened
> The imperial troops in loud and vulgar language.
> No day was free from battle and attack;
> Beneath the towering walls they traded blows,
> And black blood flowed from the exchange of wounds.
> So missiles, rocks and arrows that were swift

Were falling like a heavy snow or hail.
Each thought to fight or kill, not of himself.
On both sides raging Mars raised great confusion.
Often in the middle of the day, the youth
Broke out and yearned to fight in open country.
And often when the dark could offer rest,
They prepared to burn the camps around the fort.
The fierce commander wished to terrify
The Cremans and confuse those hated people.
He ordered six young men to be suspended
By the neck and die upon the gallows.
When they had seen them hang, the restive youth
Lamented, and at once they built a gallows
Where in a row they hanged four captive knights.
Thus they avenged their shame. Our leader glowed
With rage and quickly ordered hostages
Whom the rebels gave some time ago in hope
Of peace be brought from everywhere to die
A wretched death before their parents' eyes.
There was a lofty tower made of beams.
Cremona had it built at great expense
So that it stood above the walls and ramparts;

CHAPTER 13. SIEGES

And rocks and arrows could be hurled below
If they could move that structure near the castle.
From this machine the king expected victory.
Against it, Crema made two catapults
Which struck, as fulling mills strike at the cloth,
Both day and night with frequent blows.
Down fell the beams and nets, the boards and lattice,
And all the things that made the tower strong.
Then no one fearing death would stand upon it.
So Frederick was consumed with rage and took
Unspeakable advice. He ordered those
Poor hostages be tied upon the tower
To suffer from the catapults' attack.
Once bound in place and facing death they cried:
"Beloved brothers, spare us please! Please spare us!
Don't stain your hands on those you gave in trust,
But if you find no other way to save
Our walls, we will not flinch to give our lives!"
And with such words they uttered sighs and groans.
What should they do? Should they hold pity back
And strike their friends or let the dread machine
Approach the walls? Now if the tower reached them,
They feared both for themselves and for their country.
But they wept for those they saw exposed to death.
Since they hesitated in returning blows,
The rectors urged them on with bitter words
To keep them busy launching rocks and missiles
And stop the enemy's approach. They thought
It best to fight and sacrifice a few
Than to permit the city to be lost.
Encouraged by this advice, they shook their torpor.
In tears they struck the bodies of their comrades
And fought to drive the tower off with missiles.
They crushed their chests, their stomachs and their heads,
And bone and mushy brain were mixed together.
It was a savage, horrid thing to see.

At such a sight, the king, who now was calm,
Pitied those exposed to unjust fate.
He moved the tower back and freed the wretches.
Too late he scorned advice he took in anger.
The besieged, who wished to bury the remains,
Asked his permission, and it was quickly granted.
They stopped the war and rested several days.
The king then planned to use the greatest force
To take his savage enemies by storm.
First he had a tortoise built, and then he ordered
Men to fill the moat. So he could move that tower
Near the rampart and destroy those hostile walls.
The knights obeyed him and began to work.
Protected by the thickness of the tortoise,
The commander took a spade as an example.
But from the walls above the eager youth
Threw torches, missiles, rocks and flying arrows.
They used what means they had to stop their foes,
But the tortoise could repel the rain of blows
And let the knights continue with their labor.
And now the column struck the wall and smashed it
To make a passage big enough to enter.
Now frightened youth within, from every corner,
Ran to hold the entrance and to block the hole
With beams and they prevented an intrusion.
The shouting from this battle shook the heavens.
In all direction rocks flew from the hands
Of men, who also loosened arrows here and there.
At length dark night restrained their savage fury.
[*Barbarossa in Italy,* ll. 2953-3058]

One of the Creman commanders called Marchesius now deserted to Barbarossa and this, together with the breaching of the wall, shattered the defenders' morale. However, the Creman leaders rallied their troops:

130. They urged them to return their thoughts to war
And stirred them up with memories of their exploits.
These words inflamed the youth, and thus revived
By this advice, they formed a battle line.
They flew out and discovered that the tortoise
Was standing unprotected where the moat
Was filled. So it was burned beneath the walls.
With spears and fearsome shouts they rushed to battle
And harassed their savage foes with all that noise.
The royal troops were quick to take up arms,
And hand to hand they forced them to retreat.
Then the high commander ordered his men to use
A great machine, so that the knights could throw
A bridge across the wall and burst upon them.
When soon they pushed the engine toward the ramparts,
The Cremans could do nothing to prevent it.
But they could keep the bridge away and stop
Audacious troops from climbing on the wall.
Now from the summit of the high machine
The soldiers threw their missiles in a cluster
That fell like lightning coming down from heaven,
And rocks struck those who wandered through the castle.
The once too happy youth became confused,
And the fort was shocked to watch its ramparts fall.
The leaders who were babbling in their terror,
Could see how many met a wretched end.
The young men, who at first were bold and ready,
Now ceased to change the guard and feared the battle.
They stopped their fierce attacks upon their foes
And spent a long time pondering what to do.
[*Barbarossa in Italy*, ll. 3080-3122]

The Creman leaders advised surrender, but the rank and file wanted to continue the struggle. But after they had been bombarded from the tower for a further seven days, they lost the will to fight and asked Barbarossa for terms. He was, no doubt, glad to be spared the heavy casualties involved in an assault, and agreed to

171

let everyone go free in return for the town. This was destroyed by Frederick's allies, the men of Cremona.

An English chronicler describes the siege of Carlisle by the Scots in 1315:

131. The king of Scotland came to Carlisle, where he compassed the city round about and besieged if for ten days, treading all the crops under foot, ravaging the suburbs with the surrounding country, and burning throughout all those parts; moreover he drove a vast spoil of cattle to feed his army, from Allerdale and Westmorland. So on each day of the siege they made an assault against one of the three city gates, and sometimes at all three together, yet never with impunity. For we cast upon them from the wall javelins and arrows and stones, in such multitude and number that they asked each other, "Do stones increase and multiply, then, within these walls?" Moreover, on the fifth day of the siege they set up an engine for casting stones hard by Trinity Church, where their king had pitched his tent and they threw great stones without intermission against the wall and the Calden gate; yet with all this they did little or no harm to the townsfolk, save only that they slew one man. For we had seven or eight such engines in the city, without reckoning other engines of war, namely, springalds, for hurling long javelins, and slings on staves for casting stones, which caused much terror and havoc among the besiegers.

CHAPTER 13. SIEGES

So in the meanwhile the Scots set up a great Belfry, like a tower, which far overtopped the town walls; whereupon the city carpenters built another tower of wood that overtopped the belfry. But the Scottish engine never came against the wall; for when men dragged it on its wheels over the wet and miry ground, there it stuck fast with its own weight, nor could they draw it forward or harm us. Moreover the Scots had made long ladders, which they had brought with them for scaling the wall in divers places, and a sow [tortoise] for undermining the town wall if possible; but neither ladders nor sow availed them. Again, they made a multitude of fascines of corn and hay to fill the water moat, that they might cross it dry-shod; and long wooden bridges that ran on wheels, which they hoped to draw so strongly and swiftly with ropes as to pass that broad moat. Yet neither could those bridges pass it; but their weight dragged them to the bottom. So on the ninth day, when all their engines were ready, they made a general assault on all the city gates; and around the whole wall manfully they came on, and our townsfolk also defended themselves like men; and likewise again on the morrow.

Now the Scots here used that same wile whereby they had taken the castle of Edinburgh; for they caused the greater part of their host to make an assault upon the eastern part of the city that they might draw the defenders thither. Meanwhile the lord James Douglas, a bold and crafty knight, with others of the bravest and most active of that army, arrayed themselves on the west, where the defenses were so high and difficult of access that no assault was expected. There they reared long ladders whereby they climbed up; and they had a great host of archers who shot so thick and close that no man might show his head over the wall. Yet, blessed be God! they found such a welcome that they and their ladders were flung to the earth; at which place and elsewhere around the wall some were slain and some taken and some wounded; yet on the English side, during that whole siege, save only that man of whom we have already spoken, there was but one man smitten with an arrow, and but few were even wounded.

So on the eleventh day, either because they had news of an English host coming to raise the siege, or because they despaired of further success, the Scots retired in confusion to their own land, leaving behind all their engines of war. [*Lanercost Chronicle*]

One of the most famous French commanders of the Hundred's Year War was Bertrand du Guesclin (c. 1315-1380). He displayed his courage before the dauphin, the future Charles v, at the siege of Melun in 1359. The place was defended by an old enemy of Bertrand's, the Bascon de Mareuil:

132. Bertrand chose a ladder and laid it on his neck, and with help from others, he set it up against the wall and seized a shield to cover his head. The Bastard of Mareuil saw him coming, and cried to his men, "Good sirs, bring me the heaviest stone that you can find!"

They answered, "What are you saying? You have all that you need before you; on the one side great beams, and on the other barrels filled to the brim with stones. You cannot fail. Smite this boor who mounts so bravely. See how great and short and square he is, big and bulging like a hog in armor! Ah God! how well he would fall into the moat, and how his heart would burst with the fall! Give him good measure, for in very truth he is like a Paris street porter, all bloated under his canvas slop!"

Meanwhile Bertrand came up. With his shield at his neck and a good blade in his hand, he cried aloud to the Bastard of Mareuil, "Ho, Bastard! Let me come to the battlements and I will prove that you have no right to command here! Or come down into this alder grove, and there we will fight with a right good heart!" To this the Bastard gave no answer, but discharged a mighty herring barrel full of stones plump upon Bertrand as he mounted his ladder. So heavy

was the blow that the ladder broke, and Bertrand fell head-
long to the ground. Head first plunged he into the moat,
where he had leisure to drink his fill. Thus he remained a
while with his two feet in the air. Then came a squire who
took him by the feet and dragged him from the water. Out
came Bertrand's head all covered with mud; so stunned was
he that he did not know where he was; truth to say, he seemed
more dead than alive. They took him thence and laid him
for his comfort within a warm dungheap, until he came to
himself again and stretched his limbs. [Cuvelier, *Life of
Bertrand du Guesclin*]

The only sure way to take a fortress was to blockade it until
starvation forced its garrison to surrender. But for this, the besiegers needed plenty of time, ample supplies and enough strength to
drive away any relieving army. Edward III of England had all these
things when he laid siege to Calais after the great victory at Crécy.

The English arrived before Calais in September 1346. The town
was heavily fortified, as well as having the sea on one side and
marshes on the other. The garrison was commanded by Jean de
Vienne, one of France's most able soldiers. It would be impossible
to carry the place by assault, so the English resigned themselves to
a long siege and built a hutted camp, which they called Villeneuve-
le-Hardi, or Newtown the Brave. Several noble ladies, including
Queen Philippa, came from England to join their menfolk. Geoffrey
le Baker describes the siege:

133. The king made wide ditches round his camp, and brought
a fleet to the mouth of the harbor, so that the French could
not attack his men or provide the besieged with supplies by
sea. Then the king kept a great fleet for besieging the town,
and did not allow it to leave. The Norman pirates captured at
sundry times fifteen of his ships, great and small, some of
which they took for their own use, and others they burnt.

The king was unwilling to make an attack, knowing that
it was not possible to fight his enemies without peril, in view
of the high walls and deep ditches. Moreover, he could not

construct siege machines against the town, so that the walls could be shaken and cast down by catapults, for there was no firm ground on which the machines could be placed. Besides this, even if the walls should be destroyed, the ditch was deep and daily filled with salt water, and could easily be defended against all comers. Therefore the king abstained from attack and bombardment of the walls, calculating that hunger, which enters closed doors, could conquer the pride of the besieged.

The siege continued from the feast of the Nativity of the Virgin [Sept. 8] through the whole winter and a great part of the following summer, until on the Monday before the feast of St. John the Baptist [June 24], the tyrant of the French [Philip iv] came to the castle of Guines, swearing he would raise the siege either by war or by peace or else he would, in spite of the English, revictual the besieged. Then he approached with his army to within a mile of the English force; and having sought a truce, he sent the duke of Athènes and the counts of Bourbon and Armagnac. They negotiated with the duke of Lancaster and the earls of Northampton and Huntingdon about a truce, but could not win the assent of the English. So, after warlike tournaments, both parties went back to their tents. On the second day, the tyrant sought to fix a day of

battle to which the king of England agreed.

Meanwhile, the besieged made their distress clear to the tyrant of the French by signals; for on his first arrival they put up his banner on the chief tower of the castle and adorned the towers with the banners of the dukes and counts of France; and shortly after dark they raised a clear light with a great clamor of trumpets, drums and clarions. The next night they raised a flame, but lower than before, with a clamor of middling strength. On the third night they displayed a light which the French could hardly see, with humble submissive voice; and when it had been shown for an hour, they let it fall into the ditch of the castle; by this they signified that their power to protect the town was ended.

The day of battle approached, for which 17,000 men from England and the Teutonic League in the pay of the king assembled. Wherefore on 2 August, the tyrant of the French, seeing the king's power increased so much, went away at dawn. On leaving, he set fire to his tents, which was a melancholy sign to the besieged that he did not dare to help them, but was foolishly withdrawing. As he did so, the duke of Lancaster and the earl of Northampton harassed the rearguard, causing casualties and taking prisoners.

When the garrison of Calais discovered the flight of the wicked tyrant of the French, they threw his standard from the tower into the ditch. The following Saturday, their captain, a knight who had much experience in military affairs called Jean de Vienne, opened his gates and, seated on a little nag, for gout prevented him from walking, with a rope round his neck, came to the king. Other knights and burgesses followed on foot, bareheaded and bare-footed, also having ropes round their necks. The captain asked the king mercy and brought him the sword of peace, by which he might give good judgments and spare the lowly and humble the proud. [Geoffrey le Baker, *Chronicle*, 1347]

The surrender was followed by an incident made famous by Froissart. He states that six burgesses came with ropes round their necks, but that, in spite of their humble submission, Edward III was not inclined to show mercy:

134. Then the noble queen of England flung herself on her knees before her lord the king and said, "Ha, dear sir, since I have crossed the sea hither in great peril, as you know, I have not made one request nor asked one gift of you. Now I beg of you the gift that for the sake of the Son and Blessed Mary and for love of me, you will have mercy on these six men."

The king hesitated and looked at the good lady his wife, on her knees before him and in tears. His heart softened for he would rather not have been angry where she was, and said, "Ha, madame, I wish you were somewhere else. You pray so earnestly that I dare not refuse the gift you ask; no matter how unwilling I may be, I grant it you and do with it as you please."

The brave lady answered, "Very great thanks!" Then she arose and had the six burgesses set on their feet and took away the ropes from their necks and led them with her to her hostel. And in the morning, she gave each six nobles and had them led out of the army by Monsieur d'Aubrecicourt and Monsieur Paon de Roet, as far as they could and until it seemed to the two knights that they would be out of danger. [*Chronicles*]

The inhabitants of Calais were spared a massacre, but Edward expelled most of them from their homes and peopled the town with settlers from England. Calais was to remain in English hands for over two hundred years.

CHAPTER 13. SIEGES

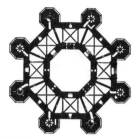

IDEAL CASTLE PLANS

CASTEL DEL MONTE, near Andria in Apulia, Italy (plan, above and elevation, left), offers an example of the classically inspired symmetrical fortress. It was designed by Emperor Frederick II Hohenstaufen as a hunting lodge c. 1240. Its hilltop location and octagonal ring of towers offered a variation on the fortresses of the Mediterranean inherited from the Romans and Byzantines.

MONTEALEGRE CASTLE in Castile, Spain (plan, right and elevation, below) shows the influence of Arabo-Byzantine fortifications.

In both instances the regular terrain of the sites allowed defenders to take advantage of a system of projecting towers to set up deadly cross fires against the siege ladders and the battering rams of attackers.

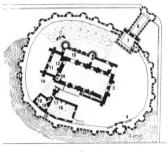

IRREGULAR PLANS: The CASTLE OF COUNTS OF FLANDERS in Ghent (above) and CORFE CASTLE in Dorset, demonstrate both the ability of medieval military architects to suit defenses to their natural sites and the evolving nature of most medieval fortifications.

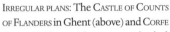

GHENT was brought to its present state c. 1180. CORFE, built c. 950, was expanded under the Normans and again, in stages, during the 13th century.

Here both castles make use of the donjon/enceinte system. The donjon, or central keep, consisted of the lord's tower, living quarters and service areas. This was enclosed by the enceinte (circuit wall) that used the site's natural defenses as a second perimeter. It enclosed an area for military excercises (lists) and provided protection for local dependents and their goods in time of war.

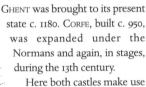

CHAPTER 13. SIEGES

TOWERS: The chief means of a castle's defense was, of course, its towers: gate, bastion, and circuit towers. Here three examples provide some idea of what a besieger would have encountered attempting to scale or breach the walls of a late medieval castle.

DONNINGTON CASTLE GATEHOUSE (above), Berkshire, was built c. 1390. The massive structure, with its twin towers, guarded the castle entrance.

The strong tower keep at the Benedictine ABBEY OF MONTMAJOUR (right) NE of Arles in southern France, was built in 1369, as protection against the mercenary Great Companies. It stands 26 meters high, and is a fine example of a tower built to withstand any weapon but protracted siege.

The 13th-century central tower of the ROCCA SCALIGERA at Sirmione (above) on Lake Garda stands 29 meters high and demonstrates a typically northern Italian system of machicolation (a projecting parapet supported by brackets) with openings below to pour molten liquids and shoot projectiles. It is surmounted by a type of crenellation also typical of the region, with mitered merlons (raised portions).

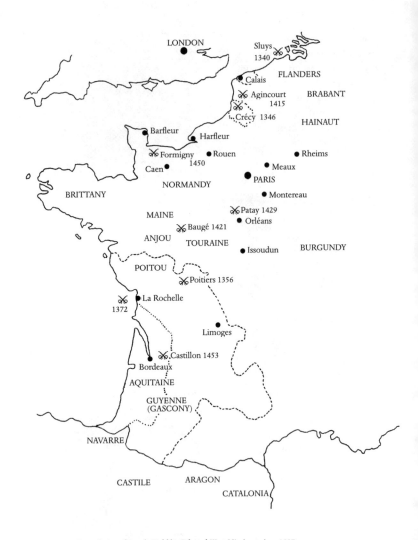

LONDON

Sluys
1340

Calais

FLANDERS

�֍ Agincourt
1415

BRABANT

✗Crécy 1346

HAINAUT

Barfleur

Harfleur

✗ Formigny
1450

Rouen

Rheims

Caen

Meaux

NORMANDY

PARIS

BRITTANY

Montereau

MAINE

✗ Patay 1429

Orléans

✗ Baugé 1421

ANJOU

TOURAINE

POITOU

Issoudun

BURGUNDY

✗ Poitiers 1356

✗
1372

La Rochelle

Limoges

✗ Castillon 1453

Bordeaux

AQUITAINE

GUYENNE
(GASCONY)

NAVARRE

CASTILE

ARAGON

CATALONIA

.... Boundaries of Lands Held by Edward III at His Accession 1327

------- Boundaries of Lands Ceded to Edward III by the Treaty of Brétigny 1360

FRANCE DURING THE HUNDRED YEARS WAR

CHAPTER 14
HENRY V IN FRANCE
1415-1422

So MANY WARS were fought during the Middle Ages that a generalized account of them would have little meaning. What follows is
a case study. It describes the wars of Henry v, who gained much
fame from his own deeds, and even more, posthumously, from
Shakespeare's play about him. These campaigns were just an episode in the so-called Hundred Years' War between England and
France, which lasted, in fact, from 1337 to 1475.

The conflict began because the French kings claimed suzerainty
over the duchy of Aquitaine, in south-west France, which belonged
to the king of England, then Edward III, while Edward made a
fanciful counter-claim to the throne of France.

At first, the war went well for the English. They won a naval
victory, Sluys, in 1340 and a great land battle, Crécy, in 1346. Then,
in 1356, the king's son, Edward, the Black Prince, won the battle of
Poitiers and captured the French king, John II. In 1360, the French
were forced to accept the Treaty of Brétigny, which greatly increased the king of England's possessions in France.

Brétigny marked the peak of the English fortunes. The war was
resumed, and the French, under the command of Bertrand du
Guesclin, adopted new tactics. They attacked isolated groups of
English troops, but they avoided pitched battles by taking refuge
in fortified towns, when threatened, and they cleared the countryside of food. Hunger, disease and steadily mounting casualties
gradually destroyed the English armies, so that when Edward III
died in 1377, he had lost most of his lands in France.

As we have seen, Edward was succeeded by his grandson, Richard
II, who refused to prosecute the war, even signing a 28-year truce

in 1396 and marrying a French princess. Henry IV, who usurped Richard's throne, had so many domestic problems that he could not embark on any foreign adventures. His successor, Henry V, felt safer, but he thought it would be wise to secure the support of his nobles by leading them on a campaign in France. Conditions there encouraged him, for the French king, Charles VI was, much of the time, insane, one of his delusions being that he was made of glass and very likely to be broken. Further, the French nobles were divided. There was a faction led by John the Fearless, duke of Burgundy, and another led by the Count Bernard VII of Armagnac.

Though he was determined on war, Henry was obliged to go through the diplomatic motions of securing peace. All that was necessary was to make his conditions so impossible that the French would never accept them. He demanded vast territories, enormous sums of money, and the hand of the French king's daughter in marriage. This is an English version of the negotiations. It contains the story which inspired Shakespeare to write the scene in which Henry receives a gift of tennis balls from the dauphin:

> 135. King Henry, conspicuous for the nobility of his character, in the second year of his reign sent to France certain ambassadors in state, that is, a bishop, two doctors and two knights in fitting array. They held a conference with the king of France and his council about a marriage to be solemnly celebrated between Henry, king of England, and the noble lady Catherine, daughter of the king of France. But these ambassadors had only a short discussion with the French on this matter without reaching any conclusion consistent with the honor or convenience of our king, and so they returned home. For these Frenchmen, puffed up with pride and lacking in foresight, hurling mocking words at the ambassadors of the king of England, said foolishly to them that as Henry was but a young man, they would send him little balls to play with and soft cushions to rest on until he should have grown to man's strength. When the king heard these words he was much moved and troubled in spirit; yet he addressed these short, wise and honest words to those

standing around him: "If God wills, and if my life shall be prolonged with health, in a few months I shall play with such balls in the Frenchmen's court-yards that they will lose the game eventually and for their game win but grief. And if they shall sleep too long on their cushions, I will awake them before they wish it, from their slumbers at dawn by beating on their doors." [John Strecche, *Chronicle for the Reign of Henry V*]

In 1415, Henry gathered an army of invasion, which was to embark from Southampton. As always, estimates of the size of the army vary, but it would seem to have been about 9,000 strong. It is said that a fleet of 1,500 ships gathered in the Solent, a figure which some modern authorities have accepted. It is, however, suspect, as it seems to be the stock number for any invading fleet. Moreover, if the size of the army was indeed 9,000, there would have been no more than six soldiers to a ship, on average. This seems absurd, even when allowance is made for all the horses, siege engines, cannon and stores that had to be carried. Some of the largest ships of the late Middle Ages could carry 1,000 passengers with their cargo.

Henry's plan was to seize Harfleur at the mouth of the River Seine, and use it as a base for an advance on Paris. The English sailed on 11 August and landed near Harfleur three days later. They then invested the town, which made such a spirited resistance that it did not surrender until 22 September. By that time, many of the English had died of dysentery and many more had been sent home, too sick to fight. When, finally, he did take Harfleur, Henry had to give it a garrison of 1,000 men. That left him an army of about 6,000 and the problem of what to do with it.

To advance on Paris with such a small force would have been folly. On the other hand, to return to England was unthinkable. Henry had made massive preparations, raised large sums of money, as well as high hopes, and had made extravagant claims on France. Were he to abandon the campaign after the capture of one small town the loss of prestige would have been disastrous. Eventually, it was decided to march through Normandy to Calais, which would at least be a convincing display of strength. Moreover, it seemed

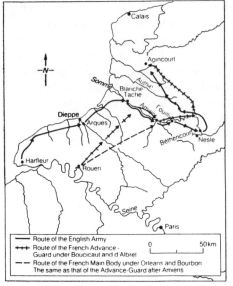

Route of the English Army
Route of the French Advance -
Guard under Boucicaut and d Albret
Route of the French Main Body under Orleans and Bourbon
The same as that of the Advance-Guard after Amiens

0   50 km

probable that the French would not try to stop such a march, since they had not come to the aid of Harfleur. Henry believed that their dissensions were preventing them from mustering an army against him.

The army left Harfleur on 6 October. It would have to cross several rivers before reaching Calais, but only the Somme was a serious obstacle. Henry hoped to cross it at the Blanche Tache ford, as his great-grandfather, Edward III, had done during the Crécy campaign. But as the English were drawing near the river, they took a prisoner who told them that the ford had been made impassable with pointed stakes and that there was, moreover, a large force guarding it. Henry led his army towards the headwaters of the river, followed by a French army on the opposite bank. Eventually, the English came to a large loop in the river, which they cut across, so gaining on their enemies, who had to go round the outside of the bend. The English were unwelcome guests, so in order to be rid of them, some peasants directed them to two fords, one at Béthencourt and the other hard by at Voyennes. The causeways leading to the fords had been broken, but the English repaired them and crossed the river unopposed. That was on 19 October. The two armies now marched in the direction of Calais, roughly parallel to each other, the French trying to head off the English. On 2 October, they succeeded. The English, tired and famished, found their way blocked by an enormous army.

CHAPTER 14. HENRY V IN FRANCE

Battle was joined the following day. The engagement was described by the unknown author of a life of Henry v, who was almost certainly present:

136. And when on the following day, Thursday, we were descending the valley towards the River of the Swords, the king was told by scouts and cavalry skirmishers that there was a powerful adversary numbering many thousands on the other side of the river, almost a league to our right. We therefore crossed the river as fast as we could, and when we reached the crest of the hill on the other side, we saw emerging from the valley about a mile from us, hateful swarms of Frenchmen, who appeared to us to be an incomparable multitude in their columns, lines and divisions. They took up their position just over half a mile ahead of us, filling a broad field like an innumerable swarm of locusts, having a small valley between us and them.

Meanwhile our king was encouraging his army courteously and bravely, marshaling them into lines and wings, as if they were to go at once into battle. And then everyone who had not previously cleared his conscience by confession, put on the armor of penitence. And among other sayings which I noted then, a certain knight, Sir Walter Hungerford, wished to the king's face that in addition to the small band which he had there he could have had ten thousand of the better archers of England, who would have been glad to be with them. The king replied: "Thou speakest as a fool, for by the God of Heaven in whose grace I trust and in whom is my firm hope of victory, I would not have one more than I have, even if I could. Dost thou not believe that the Almighty can through this humble little band overcome the pride of these Frenchmen, who boast of their numbers and their strength?"

And when the enemy in position saw and considered the disposition and fewness of our troops, they betook themselves to a field beyond a certain wood, which lay near to the left between us and them where was our road. So our king, thinking they might go round the wood to attack him along the road, or else might go round woods further away in the neighborhood and surround us from all sides, at once moved his lines and he always stationed himself to face the enemy.

And when at last we were at the last rays of light, and darkness fell between us and them we still stood in the field and heard our foes, everyone calling as the manner is, for his comrade, servant and friend, dispersed by chance in so great a multitude. Our men began to do the same, but the king ordered silence throughout the whole army, under penalty of the loss of horse and harness in the case of a gentleman, and of the right ear in the case of a yeoman or below, with no hope of pardon, for anyone who might presume to break the king's order. And he at once went in silence to a hamlet nearby, in a place where there were only a few houses; most of us had to rest in gardens and orchards, through a night of pouring rain. And when our enemies considered the quietness of our men and our silence, they thought that we were struck with fright at our small numbers and contemplated flight during the night; so they established fires and strong watches throughout the fields and routes. And as it was said they thought they were so sure of us that they cast dice that night for our king and nobles.

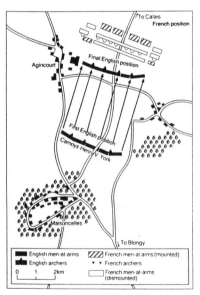

And on the morrow, Friday the feast

of Saints Crispin and Crispiana, 25 October, the Frenchmen, at dawn organized themselves into lines, battles and wedges, and took up their position facing us in the field called Agincourt, through which lay our route to Calais, in terrific multitude; and they set squadrons of horsemen in many hundreds on either side of their front lines, to break our line and the strength of our archers. The front line was composed of dismounted men made up of all the noblest and choicest of their forces, who in the forest of spears were by estimation thirty times more numerous than our men. But their rear lines were all on horseback and compared with our men they were an innumerable multitude.

And meanwhile our king prepared himself for the field, after hearing lauds and masses, and arranged his small numbers in one "battle," placing his vanguard as a wing to his right with the duke of York in command and the rearguard as a wing to his left under Lord Camoys. Interspersed among the line were wedges of archers, whom the king ordered to affix stakes in front of them, as he had ordered earlier, to stop the attacks of the horsemen.

And when much of the day had been consumed and both armies had stood and had not moved a foot, the king, seeing that the opposing army was abstaining from the attack which had been expected, either to cause us to break our order, or to strike terror into our hearts because of their numbers, or because they expected more reinforcements to arrive, and knowing our shortage of food would conquer us by hunger, ordered his men to move towards the enemy, sending orders to the baggage train of the army to follow up close so that they should not fall as booty to the enemy. After the king had estimated that all his baggage had come up to his rear, he advanced towards the enemy, with his men, in the name of Jesus and of the glorious Virgin and St. George, and the enemy moved towards him.

And when they came near enough to attack, the French horsemen posted on the sides rushed against our archers on both flanks of our army; but quickly, God willing, they were compelled to retreat by the showers of arrows and to flee behind their lines, except the large numbers whom the points of the stakes or the sharpness of the arrows stopped from flight. The crossbowmen of the enemy, who were behind the men at arms and on their flanks, fell back in face of the strength of our archers after the first draw, which was too hasty and injured only a few of our men.

But the French nobles who had first approached in line, divided themselves into three columns, either through fear of the arrows or to penetrate more quickly our force to the banners, attacked our forces at three places where there were banners; and at the first clash they met our men with such a fierce impact that they were compelled to fall back for almost the distance of a lance. And then the battle grew hotter and our archers shot their arrows through the flanks of the enemy, the battle continually renewing. And when their arrows were exhausted, they seized axes, swords and lances from those who were lying on the ground, and beat down, wounded and killed the enemy with them. And the just Judge who wished to strike down the proud multitude of the enemy with the thunderbolts of vengeance broke their power. No-one had time to receive them as captives, but almost all of them without distinction of persons, when they fell to the ground struck down by our men or by those following them, I know not by what hidden judgment of God, were killed without intermission. For when some of them slain at the start of the engagement fell in front, such was the indisciplined violence and pressure of the host behind that the living fell on the dead, and others falling on the living were killed in turn; and so in the three places where there was a concentration of our forces, the piles of dead and those crushed in between grew so much that our men climbed on these heaps which grew higher than a man and slew those below with swords, axes and other weapons. And when at last after two or three hours the vanguard was cut up and worn out, and the rest were forced into flight, our men began to sort these heaps and separate the living from the dead, intending to keep the living as property to be ransomed. But behold! at once, we know not by what wrath of God, a cry arose that the enemy's rearguard of cavalry in overwhelming numbers had repaired the enemy line and was coming against our small and tired band. And so they killed their prisoners with swords without any distinction of persons, except for the dukes of Orléans and Bourbon and other illustrious persons in the royal entourage, and a few others, lest the captives should be our ruin in the coming battle.

But after a little while the troops of the enemy, having tasted the bitterness of our weapons, and at our king's approach, left the field of blood to us, by God's will, with carts and many other wagons filled with victuals, and spears, lances and bows.

Of the French there were according to their own enumeration more than 60,000 bearing the sword, whereas the number of our small company of fighters did not exceed 6,000 men. Of this multitude there fell the dukes of Bar, Brabant and Alençon, five counts, more than 90 barons and bannerets, whose names are given in the book of records, and more than 1,500 knights according to their own computation, and between 4,000 and 5,000 other gentle folk, almost the whole nobility of French chivalry.

And of the rest there were captured the dukes of Orléans and Bourbon, the earls of Richmond, Vendôme and Eu, and also that most valiant knight the Lord Boucicault, the marshal of France, but few other gentlefolk. But there was great joy amongst our people and great astonishment, because of our small forces there were found dead on the field not more than nine or ten persons, beyond the illustrious and wise prince the Lord Edward, duke of York, and the Lord Michael, earl of Suffolk, a vigorous young man, and two newly created knights, who fell in the line of battle. Therefore our England has cause for joy and cause for grief; for joy because of a great victory and the salvation of our men, for grief because of the suffering and death of Christians. [*Gesta Henrici Quinti*]

On the French side, the two most senior officers, Jean Boucicault, marshal of France, and Charles d'Albret, constable of France, had been urging their fellows to adopt the tactics which du Guesclin had used with such success against the armies of Edward III. These were to strip the countryside of food and harass the enemy whenever possible, but to withdraw into walled towns if there was serious danger and to avoid battle at all costs. Such advice, though, went against the code of chivalry, and most of the French nobles were anxious to show their prowess in battle. However, when they did confront the English, they were persuaded not to rush at once into a suicidal attack. Instead, they stood their ground and waited, which gave Henry a problem. He could hardly retreat, for it is always difficult to disengage when an enemy is close. He could not remain where he was, because his army was short of food. To attack would have been folly, since English tactics only worked well in defense. Henry's answer was to move forward as if for the attack, and hope that this would provoke the French. Fortunately for the English, it did.

Being a sycophant, the author of the *Gesta* does not mention that the massacre of the prisoners was ordered by Henry. This killing of unarmed men has caused revulsion, though for different reasons. The massacre of prisoners was routine, but normally only the rank and file died. At Agincourt, all save the most important of the nobles were killed, which meant the loss of many valuable ransoms, and it was this which contemporaries found disgusting.

The English were too weak to exploit their victory, so they continued their march to Calais and returned home. Henry, unlike the Black Prince who waited on the captive king of France after Poitiers, had made his distinguished captives wait on him. He now subjected them to the indignity of taking part in a triumphal procession through London.

The whole of 1416 and much of the following year were taken up with complicated negotiations. Finally, Henry made an alliance with the duplicitous and unreliable John the Fearless, duke of Burgundy. In August, Henry left for France with a force of some 10,000 men, carried, as usual, in a fleet of 1,500 vessels. By early in 1418, the English had occupied much of Normandy. Meanwhile, the Burgundians took Paris and captured poor, mad Charles VI. John the Fearless now began negotiations with the Armagnacs, offering to cooperate with them against the English. Undeterred, Henry continued with his conquest of Normandy and in January 1419, its capital, Rouen, surrendered to him.

The English now took Pontoise, which brought them close to Paris, and even allowed them to cut off some of the city's supplies. This gave new urgency to the talks between the dauphin and the duke of Burgundy, who agreed to meet and plan joint action. This was to be done at Montereau, and as the two men were suspicious of each other, they were to confer in an enclosure on the town's bridge, each bringing only a few followers. During the meeting, John the Fearless was assassinated, which ended any hope of cooperation between the Armagnacs and the Burgundians. John's successor, Philip, at once made an alliance with Henry V.

The Burgundian alliance meant that Henry was able to dictate his terms to the government of Charles VI. They were set out in the Treaty of Troyes of May 1420. In the first place, Henry was to marry Charles's daughter Catherine, which was no hardship as he found her most attractive. Secondly, Henry was to inherit the throne of France when Charles died. Thirdly, because of Charles's "various infirmities," Henry was to become regent of France and govern the country in the name of his father-in-law. The one problem with this splendid settlement was that most of France was in the control of the dauphin and his allies, the Armagnacs. Henry undertook to regain this territory.

Henry and Catherine were married in June 1420 and went to England for Catherine's coronation. Then, in the spring of 1421, the royal couple made a lengthy tour of England:

137. From the cities they visited the king and queen received precious gifts of gold and silver from the citizens and prelates of the towns. Moreover after this, when the king had

reached London, he at once summoned a parliament to Westminster, and the archbishop of Canterbury held a convocation of the clergy in which a tenth and a half were granted by the clergy. And in the same parliament the king asked for and received a fifteenth and a half from the inhabitants of the realm. Moreover the king demanded and received from the more powerful men of the realm, such as merchants and bishops, abbots and priors, a great loan of money. [John Streeche, *Chronicle*]

Early in 1421, Henry had bad news from France:

138. At Easter, the duke of Clarence [Henry's brother] had been found by his enemies near Baugé, and would not rest even though it was Easter Eve. Gilbert Umfraville, marshal of France, came up to Baugé with only five horsemen and from good knowledge counseled the duke to keep the service of God and the Church during that season, and to seek out his foe after the festival. But the duke answered, "If you are afraid, go home and keep the churchyard. For you have been with the king too long to make me lose my reputation and my name; you have always gained a reputation and I have none, so you would lose me my fame by inaction."

Upon this, Umfraville said, "My lord, you have no adequate force to fight thus hastily with the enemy. Your men do not know how or when to bring you reinforcements; for truly my cousin Gray and I have here only ten men and no more, but still you shall never say we left you so." So they rode forth, chiding each other on the way until they crossed over the bridge to Baugé, where their enemies were assembled in battle array. There they alighted and fought with them at once. The duke was slain there that day, and with him were slain the earl of Umfraville, and Sir John Gray, the earl of Tancarville, Lord Roos, and Sir John Lumley, and many others. The earls of Huntingdon and Salisbury were taken prisoner and put to great ransom, and lay a long time in prison in France. The English reinforcements came when all was over and rescued the dead men where they lay, and brought the lords home who were laid upon the field that day, and buried them in England. [John Hardyng, *Chronicle*]

Here we see the code of chivalry leading Englishmen to defeat and death. The reinforcements were archers, and it was folly on Clarence's part to have fought without them, but he was unwilling to wait for such humble men.

On hearing of Baugé, Henry hurried back to France. In October 1421 he laid siege to the town of Meaux, but it did not surrender until May of the following year. Meanwhile, many of Henry's army had died of dysentery, and he, too, had contracted the disease. Probably as a result of this he died on 31 August 1422, aged 35.

Charles VI died on 11 October, cheating his son-in-law of the throne of France by six weeks.

CHAPTER 15
THE NEW WARFARE

ORGANIZATION

When Henry v died, his son, Henry vi, was a child of two, but the English had able commanders and continued with the conquest of Dauphinist France. They were, however, checked by Joan of Arc who, in 1429, relieved the city of Orléans and won a dashing victory at Patay. She also secured the coronation of the dauphin as Charles vii at Rheims. This was a symbolic gesture of some importance, because Rheims was the traditional place for the coronation of French kings and, moreover, the city was deep in enemy territory. Though she was captured the following year, she had halted the English advance and prepared the way for Charles vii to expel his enemies from France.

Charles reorganized his armies, equipping them well and employing paid professionals. The chronicler Jacques Chartier wrote:

> 139. The king of France imposed such good order on the conduct of his men-at-arms that it was a fine thing. For he caused all those men-at-arms to be equipped with good and sure armor and weapons; that is to say, the men-at-arms were all armed with good cuirasses, armor for their limbs, swords, salets, and most of the salets were adorned with silver; also with lances carried by pages of the men-at-arms, each of whom had three good horses, for himself, his page and his varlet, being armed with a salet, jacket, dirk, hauberk or brigandine, axe or bill. And each of the men-at-arms had two mounted archers, armed mostly with brigandines, leg harness, and salets.
>
> And these men-at-arms were paid each month, so that they dare not venture to take any people of the countryside

prisoners, nor to take or ransom any beast whatever it was nor to seize any victuals without paying for them, except only from the English or their adherents.

The war was conducted in masterly fashion by the count of Dunois, lieutenant of the king, with many other men-at-arms, great lords, knights and squires, who all notably, each one according to his duty, subjected themselves to great labors, travails, dangers, discomforts, pains and perils of their bodies. [*Chronique française du roi de France Charles VII*]

FIREARMS

Another important development was that the French made ever increasing use of firearms. Early guns were not very effective,

since they were made like barrels, that is, of metal strips bound round with hoops. As a result, they could not take a heavy charge without risk of bursting. Then, early in the fifteenth century, there were advances in metallurgy, so that guns could be cast in one piece. Also, in 1429, the powder mill was invented, which produced grains of gunpowder containing all the three ingredients of gunpowder, that is, carbon, sulfur and saltpeter. Formerly, these ingredients had been mixed on the battlefield

The English were given a hard lesson at the siege of Orléans when their commander, the earl of Salisbury, was mortally wounded in the face by a cannon ball. The full story of what was supposed to have happened delighted the people of Orléans. According to the legend, a boy was wandering round the battlements when he came upon a loaded gun that was, for some reason, unattended. He could not resist applying the red hot iron to the touch hole, as he had seen the crew doing, and the gun went off. At the time, Salisbury was standing at a window. He had previously ordered the destruction of the church of Notre Dame de Cléry so now, in revenge, the Virgin guided the shot towards him. It hit his head, just as a servant was saying, "My lord, behold your city."

The English did not neglect firearms, but they had so much faith in their archers that they did not adopt them with as much enthusiasm as the French. They paid a heavy price for this. In 1449 they lost the battle of Formigny because their archers were so plagued by some French guns that they were forced to break ranks and were ridden down by the French cavalry. Firearms also helped decide the last great battle of the Hundred Years War, which was Castillon in 1453. The English attacked a French army in its camp. Jacques Chartier described the battle:

> 140. In the same year, the thirteenth day of July, the French laid siege to the town of Castillon, on the river Dordogne. At first there were sent to start the siege a great company of men-at-arms, to the number of 1,600 or 1,800, and the archers. There, too, were the greater and lesser artillery of the king, under the control of Master Jean Bureau and his brother, Gaspard Bureau, who had in their company 700 gunners. When this had come to the knowledge of Lord Talbot, he at once left Bordeaux in great haste, accompanied by 800 to 1,000 English combatants on horseback. After him came from 4,000 to 5,000 Englishmen on foot.

And Talbot and his followers arrived at the siege about day break on Wednesday 17 July; and when the French knew of the arrival of Talbot, they retreated to the camp, which was well protected by ditches.

Frenchmen arrived at the camp from all parts and prepared to defend themselves. The gunners mounted their bombards, culverins and rebaudquins on the ditches towards the approaching English. While this was going on, those within the town of Castillon told Talbot that if he were to advance quickly, the French would flee. But when he arrived, he was much surprised to see the contrary, and the fine fortifications which the French had made, such ditches and artillery, so strongly emplaced, and their firm resolution to fight.

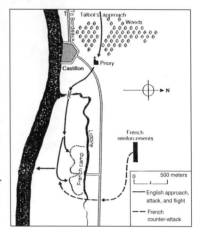

Now Talbot and his company began to arrive in great force and came up to the camp. But they found there a formidable array of valiant men, very expert in warfare. They showed themselves courageous and bold, and greeted the English bravely and pushed them back. This astonished them very much, in view of the message they had received from the defenders of the town.

Then began a great and terrible assault, with acts of great bravery on both sides, hand-to-hand fighting, and marvelous struggles with axes, guisarmes, lances, and many valiant blows. The struggle lasted for more than an hour, for the English kept returning to the attack with great ardor, and the French received them with great courage.

Then, some Breton reinforcements arrived. They did so well with the aid of God, that the English were put to flight and defeated. And all their banners were thrown down, and they left many dead on the field. Talbot's horse was struck by a shot from a culverine, so that it fell at once to the ground quite dead; and at the same time, Talbot was thrown under it and was at once killed by some archers. And thus died this famous and renowned English leader, who for so long had been reputed to be one of the most formidable scourges of the French. [*Chronique française du roi de France Charles VII*]

Castillon was a victory not only for the French, but for firearms. The English archers, who had won so many victories, were at last outmoded by a new technology at which their enemies excelled.

SIEGES

The improved artillery was even more effective for sieges than it was in the field. For most of the Middle Ages, the advantage during sieges nearly always lay with the defense. Invariably, new types of fortification were found to combat new siege tactics. For example, when

machines for hurling heavy rocks came into service, castle build-
ers strengthened their walls with round drum towers, from which
missiles would be likely to glance. But no medieval fortifications
could withstand the new artillery, especially when it was in the
hands of experts.

Jacques Chartier describes the artillery of Charles VII of France:

141. He had a great number of great bombards, great can-
ons, veuglaires, serpentines, crapaudins, culverins, and
ribaudquins, so that never in the memory of man did a Christian king have such a numerous artillery at one time, nor so
well furnished with powder, shot and all things necessary
to approach and take towns and castles, nor had more car-
riages to drag them nor gunners more experienced to handle
them, which gunners were paid from day to day. And orga-
nizers of this artillery were Master Jean Bureau, treasurer
of France, and Gaspard Bureau, his brother, master of the
said artillery; who during these wars have suffered great
pains and were found in many perils, for they have done
well their best and have acquitted themselves well of their
duty, with satisfaction to all.

It was a marvelous thing to see the bulwarks, mounds,
ditches, moats, and mines that the Bureau brothers caused
to be made before all the towns and castles that were besieged during the war; for indeed there was not a town taken
by agreement or otherwise which could not have been taken
by assault and by force of arms, if one had wished. [*Chronique
française du roi de France Charles VII*]

As Chartier hints, towns and castles surrendered without a fight,
when they knew that Jean Bureau was conducting the siege. The
English had spent years capturing the strong places of Normandy,
slowly and painfully, one by one. Equipped with the new artillery,
the French recaptured the province in a few months.

The new warfare brought fundamental changes in society. Kings
no longer depended on the feudal levy for their armies, but employed professional soldiers. Further, while rebellious barons had

once been able to defy their monarchs from the safety of their castles, this was no longer possible. The new warfare was one of the most important reasons why the military power of the nobility was broken and why, in the sixteenth century, despotic monarchies appeared in several European countries.

CHAPTER 16
THE VICTIMS OF WAR

DURING MEDIEVAL WARS, as in all others, those who were likely to suffer the most were people who had no real interest in the conflict. A French cleric wrote a poem which examines this theme:

142. I will speak also to you of the most powerful
Of the richest, and of the greatest
Of kings, of counts and of dukes,
Who have control of kingdoms.
They plunder one another's territory and wage war,
And distress the poor people
Who pay for all the wars of their lords,
And often weep thereat and sigh.
At some time there may be a king of great power
In Germany or in France;
If one king injures the other,
The peasant who is on the soil,
Pays for the wrong some day so dearly
That he has not where to sleep at night;
Nay, even the cottage
That he had low and small
Is burned and his oxen and sheep are seized,
His sons and daughters bound,
And he himself led away a wretched prisoner
So that he is sorry to be alive.
God! how shall a Christian king
Send forth from his kingdom
Thirty thousand fighting men,
Who must leave their bereaved wives and children
At home, when they go into mortal combats

In which a thousand shall soon be slain
And never again see their country,
And as many men on the other side.
Never will the kings take heed
How many fall in battle.
Never will they make count or reckoning;
Nor does either side care what he has lost,
Provided that he has conquered the other.
[Guillaume le Clerc, *Le Besant de Dieu*, c. 1226]

In 1340 Pope Benedict XII wrote to Philip VI of France, urging him to make peace with Edward III of England:

143. And behold, most beloved son, how sorry and mournful we were when we heard, and when we hear, this; when the enemy of the human race himself and the instigator of all evils, who aspires to the extermination of human salvation, lights the fires of dissension, rancor, and hatred between you and the aforesaid king into harmful and plaguebearing flames, so that the roaring of wars gains strength all around in different parts of land and sea. Thus the innocent blood of an innumerable multitude of those saved by the shedding of the Lord's precious blood was spilled so

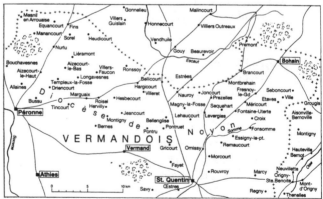

Part of Cambrai, a devastated area of northern France. The villages shown on the map were all destroyed by the English in 1340.

cruelly. Neither age nor sex was spared. Even among the infidels, in both ancient and modern times, it was reputed horror that O, misery! – children, women, the old and disabled were slain inhumanely on the point of the sword.

Blood has flowed and is flowing, and we fear that – unless divine clemency ordains otherwise – there will be an even more full and incessant blood-letting. Other dangers, damage, and scandalous perils have followed and will continue to follow from this. For now popular opinion remains unsatisfied and hostile in your kingdom of France, where the clarity of justice used to shine forth with the repression of the daring deeds of evildoers; but now delinquents, thieves, wasters, and despoilers roam about as if by official leave, and travelers and others who wish to live in peace have lost security for both their goods and persons.

Furthermore, because of the multiplication of many and unbearable tax burdens, the poor cry out, and the bread is taken right out of their hands and borne away. The rich roar, the church people are heavily and lamentably overcome, not a few asserting, as we have heard, that with almost all their incomes removed they are forced miserably to experience the opprobrium of poverty as if they are beggars. [Benedict XII, *Letters*]

SIEGES

Troops who stormed a town ran wild. The anonymous poet who described the campaigns of Frederick I in Italy told of the capture of Iseo:

> 144. It was a short but brutal thing. The sword
> Subdued them; by the sword the fort was lost.
> The victors raged and grabbed the best as loot;
> The vanquished trembled, hid and were despoiled.
> And everywhere the groans and frightful mourning
> Were mixed with fear and images of death.
> Some ran into the mountains, and some swam
> Into the lake; without their clothes or goods

They tried to flee. But those who wanted death
Burned all the plunder, even their own houses.
Thus Iseo was destroyed by fire and sword,
And leaving nothing to the conquered people,
The royal army carried off rich treasure.
The king was thought to think the thoughts of God,
And he was feared by every living being.
[*Barbarossa in Italy*, ll. 3197-3211]

During a protracted siege, the men of the garrison kept most of
the food and would not surrender until they themselves were starv-
ing. By that time, many of the civilians had died of hunger. Henry
v besieged Rouen, the capital of Normandy, from July 1418 until
January 1419 and by October there was famine in the town. John
Page, who was with the English army, described the sufferings of
the inhabitants:

145. Meat and drink and other victual
In that city began to fail.
Save clean water and plenty too,
And vinegar to put thereto.
Their bread was very nearly gone,
And flesh save horsemeat they had none,
They ate up dogs, they ate up cats;
They ate up mice, horses and rats.
For a horse's quarter lean or fat,
One hundred shillings it was at.
A horse's head for half a pound,
A dog for the same money round,
For thirty pennies went a rat,
For two nobles went a cat,
For sixpence went a mouse,
They left but few in any house.
For bread as broad as is my hand
Was worth a franc I understand.
It was very poor that they could find,
For it was made of such a kind,

CHAPTER 16. THE VICTIMS OF WAR

Not of meal and not of oats,
But of bran, as God it wots.
Then to die they did begin,
All that rich city within.
They died so fast on every day
That men could not them in earth lay.
Even if a child should otherwise be dead,
The mother would not give it bread.
Nor would a child to its mother give.
Everyone tried himself to live
As long as he could last.
Love and kindness both were past.
[John Page, *The Siege of Rouen*]

To save food, the garrison of Rouen drove many of the poor out of the city. The English would not allow them to pass through their lines, so they had to stay in the town ditch:

146. There men might see a great pity,
A child of two years or of three
Go about and beg his bread,
For father and mother both were dead.
And under them the water stood
And yet they lay crying after food.
Some had starved in that place to death,
And some had stopped both eyes and breath,
And some were crooked in their knees
And were now lean as any trees.
You saw a woman hold in her arm
Her own dead child, with nothing warm,
And babies sucking on the pap
Within a dead woman's lap.
There men might find it last arrive
That twelve were dead to one alive.
And the dead knew nought of death
So secretly they gave up their breath
Without a noise or any cry,

As if they slept, so did they die.
[John Page, *The Siege of Rouen*]

RANSOM

During the Hundred Years War, the English were inspired, largely, by greed. The nobility hoped to capture wealthy prisoners and hold them to ransom. A French writer justified this practice:

> 147. According to law, all that a man can win from his enemy in war, he may keep. So, seeing that he holds the man's person, and by releasing him may have a ransom, why should he be blamed? Also, if a man had all his possessions with him in battle, they would, by law, be taken by his conqueror. Why, then, should the conqueror not have them before he allows his prisoner to go? Again, by written law among Christians there is the custom of taking ransom, one from another. [Honoré de Bonet, *L'Arbre de Batailles*, 1387]

At the battle of Agincourt in 1415, William, Lord Moleyns, took eight prisoners whose ransoms allowed him to build a handsome castle at Farleigh Hungerford, in Somerset. Obviously, the English ran the risk of being captured themselves. This incident happened after Poitiers, 1356, ironically a great victory for the English:

> 148. It happened that a squire of Picardy called John de Hellenes fled from the battle. At the same time there was in the field the Lord Berkeley of England, a lusty young knight, and he all alone pursued the said John. And when he had followed him for a league, John turned and came running towards Lord Berkeley, who lifted up his sword to strike the squire; but when he saw the stroke coming, he turned from it, so that the Englishman missed him. Then, as he passed, John struck Lord Berkeley on the arm, and his sword fell into the field. When he saw his sword down, he dismounted from his horse, and stooped to take his sword. At this, the French squire thrust his sword at him and through both thighs, so that the knight fell on the earth and could not

CHAPTER 16. THE VICTIMS OF WAR

help himself. And John alighted off his horse and took the knight's sword that lay on the ground and asked him if he would yield or not.

"Well," said the knight, "I am content to be your prisoner, for you have by law of arms won me." Then he swore to be his prisoner, rescue or no rescue.

The squire drew his sword from out of the knight's thighs. Then he wrapped and bound the wound and set him on his horse and brought him to Chatellerault, and there rested him for fifteen days. When he was somewhat better, he got him a litter and so brought him in comfort to his house in Picardy. There he remained more than a year, until he was completely cured. And when he left, he paid 6,000 nobles for his ransom. And so the squire was made a knight, because of the profit he had from the Lord Berkeley. [Froissart, *Chronicles*]

It was generally accepted that if a knight or a noble had to pay a ransom, then he could levy a special tax or "aid" from his peasants to meet the cost. In the unlikely event of a king being captured, then the whole country was taxed. The enormous sum which the English demanded from John ɪɪ after he was taken at Poitiers in 1356 would have beggared France, if it had ever been paid in full. Thus, while the capture of a nobleman was a misfortune for himself, it could be a disaster for his subjects.

PLUNDER AND DESTRUCTION

As well as ransom there was plunder, which all ranks might take. A chronicler said of England after Poitiers:

149. For the woman was of no account who did not possess something from the spoils of Caen and Calais, and other cities of France, such as clothing, furs, quilts and utensils. Scattered through England in every house were to be seen table-cloths and jewels, bowls of murra and silver, linen and linen cloths. [Thomas of Walsingham, *Chronicle of England*]

During the Hundred Years War, few of the English nobles wished to die gloriously so, in general, they tried to avoid battle. Their usual method of warfare was to conduct a chevauchée, or ride, a euphemism for a plundering expedition. The army descended on the French countryside, holding wealthy people to ransom and slaughtering the rest, carrying off what was worth taking and burning what remained. The following extracts describe the misery they inflicted:

150. When they found themselves in a fertile area, the English stayed three or four days until they had refreshed themselves and their horses, then rode ahead, sending their servants out to strip the land of food, often for ten leagues on both sides, and if it was well stocked, they stayed two or three days bring-

ing back to the army very many cattle. And they found much wine, more than they needed, and they wasted much of it....

The country was plentiful of everything, the granges full of corn, the houses full of riches, rich burgesses, carts and chariots, horses, pigs, sheep and other beasts; they took what they wanted and brought it back into the army. But the soldiers made no count to the king nor to any of the officers for the gold and silver that they did get, but kept that to themselves. [Froissart, *Chronicles*]

CHAPTER 16. THE VICTIMS OF WAR

151. From the Loire to the Seine the peasants have been slain or put to flight. We ourselves have seen vast empty plains absolutely deserted, uncultivated, abandoned, empty of inhabitants, covered with bushes and brambles. Indeed, in most of the thickly wooded districts, forests are growing up. [Thomas Basin, *Histoire de Charles VII*, 1425]

152. There were no cattle in the fields. No cock crowed in the night. Rabbits and hares played freely in the deserted fields, for no one dared go hunting. No travelers went along the roads, carrying their cheese and butter to market. Houses and churches were smoking ruins. Men were no longer made happy by the sight of fields full of growing grain. Instead they were saddened by nettles and thistles springing up everywhere. The pleasant sound of the bell was still heard, but warning that the enemy was coming. [Jean de Venette, *Chronicle*, 1430]

153. At this time the king of England was before Meaux and spent Christmas and Epiphany there: and all over Brie his men were pillaging everywhere; and on account of them and the Burgundians, who left nothing that they could not carry away, no one could work or sow anywhere. Often complaints were made to the English and Burgundian lords, but they only mocked and laughed and egged on their troops worse than before. Hence, most of the peasants ceased to work and were in despair and left their wives and children saying to each other, "What shall we do? Let us put everything into the hands of the devil, for it cannot matter what becomes of us. It will benefit us as much to do our worst as to do our best. The Saracens would treat us better than the Christians, so let us do the worst we can. They cannot do more to us than kill us or take us prisoner; for by the false government of traitorous rulers we have had to leave our wives and children and to flee into the woods like wandering beasts."

It is not one year or two, but fourteen or fifteen years since this tragic dance began. [*Journal d'un bourgeois de Paris,* 1422-1423]

154. The English came to Chantecoq and set fire to almost the whole countryside. They then brought the entire region under their rule. They ordered the people who were at all wealthy to pay ransom. If they did not, their goods would be seized, their houses burnt, and they themselves would be killed. Terrified by this, many people promised to give the English money and flour, oats and other food, if only they would leave them alone. They were killing many men. Some they kept in prison, threatening them with death, some they tortured without mercy.

Other people, wanting to escape, made huts in the woods. They ate their bit of bread in fear and sorrow. I was among them for I had built a hut in the wood of Cauda and here I stayed with many of my neighbors. Daily, we heard about the horrid deeds of our enemies. They burnt houses and left many dead bodies lying about the villages, as is their vile custom. One night those cursed English found my hut. They nearly took me as I slept, but by the grace of God, I managed to run away. Naked as I was, I escaped, taking with me only my tunic and my hood. I crossed the marsh and stayed there, trembling with fear and shivering with cold. I remained long enough to see my hut completely destroyed. [*Tribulations d'un religiuex*]

CHAPTER 17
THE PEACEMAKERS

THE EARLY CHURCH

Like warfare, peacemaking took many forms. In the early years of the Church the Christians were a persecuted minority so they could do little to influence events. But they did at least issue protests, like this one against boxing, which was done with knuckle dusters, not gloves, and fights to the death between gladiators:

> 155. I have seen men weighed down by bodily exercise, and carrying about the burden of their flesh, before whom rewards and chaplets are set, while the adjudicators cheer them on, not to deeds of virtue, but to rivalry in violence and discord; and he who excels in giving blows is crowned. These are the lesser evils; as for the greater, who would not shrink from telling them? Some, giving themselves up to idleness for the sake of profligacy, sell themselves to be killed; and the indigent barters himself away, while the rich man buys others to kill him. And for these the witnesses take their seats, and the boxers meet in single combat, for no reason whatever, nor does any one come down into the arena to succor. Do such exhibitions as these redound your credit? He who is chief among you collects a legion of blood-stained murderers, engaging to maintain them; and these ruffians are sent forth by him, and you assemble at the spectacle to be judges, partly of the wickedness of the adjudicator, and partly of that of the men who engage in the combat. And he who misses the murderous exhibition is grieved, because he was not doomed to be a spectator of wicked and impious and abominable deeds. The robber commits murder for the

sake of plunder, but the rich man purchases gladiators for the sake of their being killed. [Tatian, *Discourse on the Greeks*, c. A.D. 160]

When Christianity was well established, churchmen often took the lead in defending their flocks. Eadmer, bishop of Sherborne, for example, led an army against the Danes, "made great slaughter and gained the victory." St. Germanus of Auxerre (c. 378-448) had other methods:

156. He had hardly gotten home after his overseas expedition when a deputation from Armorica [modern Brittany] came with a petition to the weary prelate. For Aetius the Magnificent, who then governed the state, had been enraged by the insolence of that proud region and, to punish it for daring to rebel, had given Goar, the savage king of the Alans, permission to subdue it; and Goar, with a barbarian's greed, was thirsting for its wealth.

So one old man was matched against a most warlike people and an idolatrous king but, under the protection of Christ, he proved greater and stronger than them all. He lost no time in setting out, for all the preparations for the invasion had been made. The movement of the tribes had already begun and their iron-armed cavalry were filling all the roads. Nevertheless our bishop rode out towards them till he reached his meeting place with the king, who arrived soon after him.

Since the march was in progress when the meeting took place, the priest was opposed to a war-lord clad in armor and surrounded by his bodyguard. First, he made requests, through the medium of an interpreter. Then, as Goar disregarded them, he went on to rebuke him. Finally, he stretched out his hand, seized his bridle and halted him, and with him the whole army.

The wrath of the savage king at this was turned by God to marveling. He was staggered by such firmness, awed by such dignity and shaken by the strength of such insistent authority. The panoply of war and the rattle of arms gave place to the courtesies of a peaceful interview. Laying aside his arrogance the king dismounted and entered upon negotiations which ended by satisfying, not the desires of the king, but the requests of the bishop. The king and his army camped peacefully where they were and he gave the most solemn assurances of peace on condition that the pardon which he himself had thus granted to the Armoricans was asked also of the emperor or Aetius. Meanwhile the mediation of the bishop, and his holiness, had restrained a king, recalled an army and delivered a province from devastation. [Constantius of Lyons, *Life of St. Germanus of Auxerre*, c. A.D. 480]

POPULAR PEACE MOVEMENTS

Towards the end of the tenth century, there was disorder in many parts of Europe, with nobles and, more particularly, lesser knights, victimizing defenseless people. In the absence of strong central government, bishops took the lead in organizing peace movements. One of these was the Truce of God, which tried to outlaw violence at certain times. For example, the Council of Cologne of 1083 decreed:

157. That from the first day of the Advent of Our Lord through Epiphany, and from the beginning of Septuagesima to the eighth day after Pentecost [about 160 days], and throughout the year on every Sunday, Friday and Saturday, and on the fast days of the four seasons, and on the eve and day of all the apostles, and on all days canonically set apart for fasts and feasts, this decree of peace shall be observed. [In Musto, op. cit., p. 452]

There was also the Peace of God, which aimed to protect those who were forbidden or unable to bear arms, such as women, peasants and clergy. This movement began in popular assemblies where people from all walks of life and all classes of society swore oaths to keep the peace. Ralph Glaber, a Cluniac monk, describes these meetings:

158. At the millennium of the Lord's Passion, which followed these years of famine and disaster, by divine mercy and goodness the violent rainstorms ended; the happy face of the sky began to blow with gentle breezes and by gentle serenity to proclaim the magnanimity of the Creator. The whole surface of the earth was benignly verdant, portending ample produce which altogether banished want. It was then that the bishops and abbots and other devout men of Aquitaine first summoned great councils of the whole people, to which were borne the bodies of many saints and innumerable caskets of holy relics. The movement spread to Arles and Lyons, then across all Burgundy into the furthest corners of the French realm.

Throughout the dioceses it was decreed that in fixed places the bishops and magnates of the entire country should convene councils for re-establishing peace and consolidating the holy faith. When the people heard this, great, middling and poor they came rejoicing and ready, one and all, to obey the commands of the clergy no less than if they had been given by a voice from heaven speaking to men on earth. For all were still cowed by the recent carnage, and feared lest they might not obtain future abundance and plenty.

A roll divided into headings was drawn up, giving a list of all that was prohibited, and a record of what men had, by sworn undertaking, decided to offer to Almighty God. The most important of these was that the peace should be preserved inviolate so that all men, lay and religious, whatever threats had hung over them before, could now go about their business without fear and unarmed. The robber and the man who seized another's domains were to suffer the whole rigor of the law, either by a heavy fine or corporal punishment. The holy places of all churches were to be held in such honor and reverence that if someone guilty of any crime fled there he would get off unharmed, unless he had violated the peace oath, in which case he could be seized before the altar and made to suffer the established penalty. All clerics, monks and nuns also were to be given reverence, such that those traveling with them were not to be harmed by anyone.

Such enthusiasm was generated that the bishops raised their crosiers to the heavens, and all cried out with one voice to God, their hands extended: "Peace!" This was the sign of their perpetual covenant with God. It was understood that after five years all should repeat this wonderful celebration in order to confirm the peace. In that same year there was such a plentiful abundance of corn and wine and other foods that the like could not be hoped to be obtained in the following five years. All food was cheap except meat and rare spices: truly it was like the great Mosaic jubilee of ancient times. [Ralph Glaber, *The Five Books of the Histories*, c. 1046]

Certain bishops were not happy with the peace movement, among them Adalbero of Laon, who is mentioned in the first chapter of this book. Adalbero was worried about people taking oaths since, at the very least, they were guilty of spiritual pride in assuming they had the strength to keep their word, while if they defaulted they put their souls in danger. Moreover, the movement seemed to be itself a source of anarchy, for the meetings tended to be hysterical and, more important, class distinctions were ignored. This was one reason why the doctrine of the three orders appealed to men like Adalbero, who maintained that the best guarantee of peace was a disciplined, hierarchical society, under the control of its spiritual leaders.

Eventually, the Peace of God turned into the Imperial Peace, or, in other words, it was institutionalized and became the tool of the feudal nobility, the very people against whom it had originally been directed. It now showed quite a different spirit. For example, an edict the Emperor Henry IV issued in 1103 contained the strange injunction, "If thou shalt meet thine enemy on the road and canst harm him, do so, but if he escapes to the house or castle of anyone, thou shalt let him remain there unharmed."

There were other popular peace movements during the Middle Ages. A Franciscan, Salimbene de Adam (d. c. 1288), describes the Great Alleluia of 1233:

159. This was the time of the Alleluia, as it was later to be called, a time of happiness and joy, gladness and rejoicing, praise and jubilation, of quiet and peace, with all weapons laid aside. During this time, the people of the city and the country "young men and maidens, the old with the younger" [Ps. 148:12], even the knights and soldiers, sang songs and divine hymns. And this spirit of devotion was abroad in all the cities of Italy. As I myself saw in my native city of Parma, for example, every parish devised a banner to be borne in holy procession, on which was depicted the martyrdom of its own particular saint, as, for instance, the flaying of St. Bartholomew on the banner of the parish where his church is situated – and likewise with all the others. Moreover, huge companies of men and women, boys and girls, came to the city from the villages round about with their own banners, so that they might be able to hear the preachers and give praise to God. And they sang, "voice of a god, and not of a man" [Acts 12:12], and they walked about as men saved in fulfillment of the prophetic words: "All the ends of the earth shall remember, and shall be converted to the Lord. And all the kindreds of the Gentiles shall adore in his sight" [Ps. 21:28]. And all men carried about with them tree branches and lighted candles. Furthermore, there was preaching at evening, morning, and noon, according to the prophecy, "evening and morning, and at noon, I will speak and de-clare: and he shall hear my voice. He shall redeem my soul in peace from them that draw to me; for among many they were with me" [Ps. 54:18-19]. And the crowds of people made stops in the churches and in the squares, lifting up their hands to God in praise and blessing for ever and ever; truly, they could not cease from divine praise because they were so in-ebriated with divine love. And blessed was he who could do

the most good works and could best praise God. There was no anger in them, no disturbance, no discord, no rancor. They did all things peacefully and benevolently. [Salimbene de Adam, *Chronicle*]

In 1399 the Bianchi movement suddenly appeared in northern Italy. It took its name from the white garments worn by the devotees. It was similar to the Peace of God movement in that it included all social classes and was encouraged by senior churchmen. A Genoese chronicler described it:

160. The citizens and the women of Genoa went to confession; and many sought forgiveness from one another, so that on Thursday the tenth of July many citizens and women received the Eucharist at a mass heard at dawn. After this mass, all the citizens, the nobles and advocates of the people, all the women, virgins, married women, widows, children and the greater part of the slaves went together in white clothes, and with the entire clergy also dressed in white, with crosses and the priests assigned to each group walking before them, they entered the basilica. There the archbishop of Genoa, Jacopo de Flisco, covered in a white cloth, stood mounted on his horse, with the ashes of the archprophet John the Baptist and with his holy relics.

Leaving the major church, with similar acts and ceremonies, they took a second road used for the solemnities of

the procession of Corpus Christi, and went even further, all the way to the monastery of San Tomaso and to Bisagno to the monastery of San Giovanni de Pavarono. You have to believe the innumerable people who were at this ceremony. Genoa was full of people; for many pursued peace by such means. For as they marched through the city in the ceremonies the countryfolk who had been rivals went bound together with a rope or belt.

[Demonstrations went on for nine days and nights.]

If there were the beautiful relics of saints in a church, they took their relics from that church along with wax tapers. On one of those nine days the Franciscans carried all their saints' relics through the city with a large number of the people; on another day the Dominicans did the same; and on Sunday the thirteenth of July the laypeople of Genoa who live under the Discipline in congregations and whip themselves and are called the Oratories of the Passion of God [Flagellants], whipping themselves by their own hand in memory of Jesus, did a procession through the city.

Many men and women from Genoa went to Recco, and thus they introduced those who lived on that shore to this new devotion; and so this spiritual devotion reached the eastern Riviera, all the way to the districts of Chiavari and Rapallo, where there were intense hatreds. This spiritual rite was celebrated solemnly by a multitude of people, so that the Ghibellines and Guelphs of those districts attained true peace. [Giorgio Stella, *The Annals of Genoa*, 1399]

CHAPTER 17. THE PEACEMAKERS

THE PEACE BROKERS

Popes saw it as their duty to make peace between warring states. In 1316, Pope John XXII wrote the following letters:

> 161. To our beloved son, the noble Philip, the son of the king of France of bright memory, regent of the kingdom of France and of Navarre. A special affection draws us, son, to your person and to the most Christian realm of France, in which we have our origin, and a special love affects us, so that we suggest those things that are appropriate for your salvation and that we see as clearly useful to you and the kingdom itself.
>
> Clearly, son, it is not hidden to you, since it is apparent to the whole world, how that Flemish war prolonged under the care of the enemy of peace and the sower of weeds, has disturbed the said kingdom for such a long time. Nor is it hidden how much it leads to the peril of souls, the slaughter of bodies, and the disruption of lawful life, so that the same kingdom appears so destitute that no plague is more efficient in harming it than the familiar enemy.
>
> Nor are you ignorant of how until now the sword of Gallic power had been polished and sharpened against Christ's blasphemers and for the exaltation of the faith and the spreading of the Christian religion. But now, because of this commotion and disruption, it has – for shame – become sharpened and polished for the spilling of Christian blood. Your father, inflamed with the effects of devotion, strove personally to take up the Crusade beyond the sea. But distracted into pursuing the aforementioned war while he still lived, he was unable to undertake the said voyage. Nor can you, who say that you are inclined to the same crusade and have therefore already taken up the emblem of the cross, easily arm yourself for it, since as long as the division of this war endures, you would have had, and now have, to abandon the defense of the said kingdom.
>
> Because of which, when, as we hear happily, a treaty of peace may have already been negotiated with concord between you

and the aforesaid people of Flanders – albeit it is not yet confirmed with sworn agreement – with fatherly concern we fear lest the jealous enemy of peace impede, disrupt, or disturb it with his tricks. So, warning and asking and exhorting, we lead your highness in the Lord Jesus Christ, persuading you with sound advice, that you attend to all the

Johannes der.ḟḟiȷ.

just-mentioned things with consideration, making your spirit suitable for peace, according to the example of him for whom it is proper to always have pity and to forebear, and whose compassion is described above all his works, so that you piously convert to the gentleness that you are able to muster, despite the wrath that the Flemish themselves deserve, and so that you mercifully admit these very Flemish to the shelter of your grace and to full reconciliation.

The road lies open before you. The Holy Land urgently expects your aid. God willing, it is more ready for you, and the duty of the said crusade is incumbent on you. The desire for its speedy completion urges us on, and its delay saddens us in so many ways.

162. To the noble Robert, count, and to the communes of the villages and the districts of the county of Flanders, who do not know pride and who feel solidarity with the humble. Peace in the tabernacles of the Lord is very beloved to those who love his name, but is nothing to the impious, since it is promised through the heavenly messengers to people of good will [Lk. 2:14]; but it is destroyed by the unjust and denied by evildoers.

CHAPTER 17. THE PEACEMAKERS

Indeed it has long and widely been known how once your seditious revolt arose against Philip [IV] of bright memory, the king of France, it had produced serious grievances and many injuries not only to the most Christian kingdom of France but to almost the whole world. It has sown difficulties and harvested sorrows, from which come – oh, misery – danger to the soul, slaughter to the body, the interruption of lawful life and obstacles to aiding the Holy Land, for which the king himself strove with pious intentions.

And while the said king still conducted human affairs, electing more to have mercy than to take revenge, from his innate sense of clemency, he indulged your excesses mercifully. And he liberally admitted you to the grace of his reconciliation through a concord agreed to on both sides and solemnly confirmed by the Apostolic See at the urging of both parties. You are said to have promised that you would obey this effectively through oaths exacted on this.

Since you have not observed the agreements, because of your action you have wished that we, by apostolic authority, impose sentences of excommunication on persons and interdicts on lands. Despite this, ingrates from grace, damnably, just is it is written, "you return to your vomit" [Prov. 26:11] and you have weakened peace itself through your audacious rashness, discarding the terms of the settlement and ignoring the transgressions of your oaths.

Most recently, however, after many sorrows that come on night winds, with the purification of the rosy dawn from the heavens above, it has come about, as we happily have heard, that a peace has been initiated and confirmed between Louis [X] of fresh memory, the king of France and Navarre, and you and that a treaty has been undertaken in a sure way. Despite the latter's death, we are happy to hear that you are diligently pursuing it with our beloved son, the noble Philip [V], the brother of the said king, the regent of the aforesaid kingdom.

For his singular support – after that of God – the Holy
Land sighs, exhausted with the tedium of its anxious expectation, fully desiring to seek out the good of peace and the
sweetness of quiet. But the said enemy of the human race,
the lover of quarrels, exerts himself immoderately on this
score so that he impedes the aid for the said Holy Land,
distracting the regent with civil wars.

In the Lord's name we admonish and ask and exhort the
nobility and your communities, persuading you with wholesome advice, as much as we can, that you consider all we
have said above with discernment, making straight your ways
in the Lord's eyes, and that you take care to follow the aforesaid treaty prudently and diligently and to offer the same to
the aforesaid regent so that he may be inclined to deal clem-
ently with you and admit you into the bosom of his good
graces; and at length with that treaty completed and its ex-
ecution accomplished, with peace running to meet you like
an honored mother, your name may be removed from the
list of the impious.

Otherwise, if you should presume to ignore our wholesome warnings, which God forbid, we want you to know
that we intend to advance to punishment against you. [Pope
John xxii, *Letters*]

Most of the pope's reasons for wanting peace in Europe are clear
from the letters. Other motives, not stated, was that war damaged
church property and interrupted the flow of taxes to the papal coffers.

Senior churchmen sometimes tried to prevent armies from fighting. Immediately before the battle of Poitiers in 1356, Cardinal
Talleyrand of Périgord approached the English commander, the
Black Prince and the king of France, John ii. The English, who felt
they were trapped, were inclined to listen:

163. When both lines were arrayed, in the light of dawn on
Sunday, there came to the prince a certain cardinal of
Périgord, who implored him, for the honor of God who was
crucified and the love of the Virgin, His mother, and the

respect of ecclesiastical peace, to avoid shedding Christian blood, that he would be pleased to delay the battle to give time for treating of peace; and the cardinal promised an honorable future by his intercession. The prince, who was entirely free from the will to tyranny, neither feared battle nor refused peace, but modestly agreed to the petition of the holy father. And so, through the whole of that day, assigned for making peace, the French army increased by a thousand men-at-arms and a great multitude of other people.

On the morrow, the cardinal came back and besought on behalf of the French king a year's truce, which the prince denied; at last, at the great entreaty of the cardinal, he conceded a truce to last until Christmas. The cardinal therefore demanded from the king a truce, such as the prince had accepted; the marshal of Claremont advised the king to concede this, but Marshal d'Audrehem, Geoffrey de Chargny, and Douglas the Scot opposed the idea, and the king was strongly inclined to their side. They forecast that in the common course of nature the English could not prevail, when they were so few, and were tired out by their ignorance of the countryside and their arduous journeys, against the numbers of the French soldiers who were defending their own soil and refreshed with all necessary victual. All this ought to increase their boldness against plunderers; the grace of the king who had been crowned and anointed with holy oil would then be experienced, with the benediction of the bishops of Sens and Châlons fighting under the same king. [Geoffrey le Baker, *Chronicle*]

Cardinal Talleyrand's mission failed, as many similar initiatives have done, and for much the same reasons. In the event, the English won a great victory at Poitiers, even taking the French king prisoner.

A ruler who was looking for peace might well employ a churchman as his ambassador. In 1197, the archbishop of Canterbury carried out negotiations during a war between Richard I of England and Philip II of France:

164. Hubert, archbishop of Canterbury, was ordered by the king of England to cross the sea, and he left Lambeth, returning there twenty weeks and six days later.

While in Normandy he accomplished many useful acts. He heard that the bishop of Beauvais in his twin roles of bishop and count, found girded with knightly arms according to what he boasted were the customs of his ancestors, had been captured and was held in chains by Richard I. The archbishop managed to persuade the king to keep the bishop in easier confinement. He reconciled the church of Rouen, where divine service had been suspended. He added certain clauses to the peace treaty between the king of England and Baldwin, count of Flanders. He worked hard, and in the event successfully, to restore peace between Richard and the archbishop of Rouen, as a permanent exchange was made to the church of Rouen for Les Andeleys. [Ralph of Diceto, *Images of History*, c. 1202]

Archbishop Hubert was wise enough to attempt only the possible and, as a result, he was successful.

BIBLIOGRAPHY

PRIMARY SOURCES

Amt, Emilie. *Womens Lives in Medieval Europe: A Sourcebook*. New York: Routledge, 1993.

Brie, Frederick W.D., ed. *The Brut, or the Chronicles of England*. 2 vols. London: Oxford University Press for the Early English Text Society, 1960.

Burns, Robert I., ed. *Emperor of Culture: Alfonso x the Learned of Castile and his Thirteenth-Century Renaissance*. Philadelphia: University of Pensylvania Press, 1990.

Cantor, Norman F., and Michael S. Werthman, eds. *Medieval Society 400-1450*. Arlington Heights, IL: Harlan Davidson, 1982.

Capellanus, Andreas. *The Art of Courtly Love*. New York: W.W. Norton, 1969.

Carson, Thomas, ed. and trans. *Barbarossa in Italy*. New York: Italica Press, 1994.

Chaucer, Geoffrey. *The Canterbury Tales: Done into Modern English Verse by Frank Ernest Hill*. New York: Heritage Press, 1974.

Critchlow, F.L., ed. and trans. *Chronicle of the Reign of King Pedro III of Aragon*. 2 vols. Princeton: Princeton University Press, 1928-1934.

Forster, John, ed. and trans. *The Chronicle of James I, King of Aragon*. 2 vols. London: Chapman & Hall, 1883.

Fortescue, Sir John. *The Governance of England. Otherwise Called the Difference between an Absolute and a Limited Monarchy*. Charles Plummer, ed. Oxford: Clarendon Press, 1885. Reprint, Westport, CT: Hyperion, 1986.

Frederick II of Hohenstaufen. *The Art of Falconry*. C.A. Wood and F. Marjorie Fyfe, eds. and trans. Stanford: Stanford University Press, 1943.

Froissart, Jean. *Chronicles*. J. Joliffe trans. & ed. New York: Modern Library, 1967.

Gray, Thomas. *Scalacronica: A Chronicle of England and Scotland from A.D. 1066 to A.D. 1362*. Sir Herbert Maxwell, trans. Glasgow: James Lehose and Son, 1907.

Griffiths, Ralph A., and James Sherborne, eds. *Kings and Nobles in the Later Middle Ages*. London & New York: St. Martin's Press, 1987.

Hallam, Elizabeth, ed. *Chronicles of the Age of Chivalry*. London: Weidenfeld and Nicolson, 1987.

—. *The Four Gothic Kings: The Turbulent History of Medieval England and the Plantagenet Kings Henry III, Edward I, Edward II and Edward III, Seen through the Eyes of Their Contemporaries*. New York: Grove Weidenfeld, 1987.

—. *Plantagenet Chronicles*. London: Weidenfeld and Nicolson, 1986.

Herlihy, David, ed. *History of Feudalism*. New York: Harper & Row, 1970.

Hollister, C. Warren, ed. *Medieval Europe: A Short History*. New York: Alfred A. Knopf, 1982.

Langland, William. *Piers the Ploughman*. Margaret Williams, trans. New York: Random House, 1971.

Musto, Ronald G., ed. *Catholic Peacemakers: A Documentary History*. Vol. I: *From the Bible to the Era of the Crusades*. New York: Garland Publishing, 1993.

Pere III [of Aragon]. *Chronicle*. J.N. Hillgarth and Mary Hillgarth, eds. and trans. 2 vols. Toronto: University of Toronto Press, 1980.

Radstone, V.B., ed. *The Household Book of Dame Alice de Bryene*. Ipswich: Suffolk Institute of Archaeology and History, 1931.

Salimbene da Adam. *The Chronicle of Salimbene da Adam*. Joseph L. Baird, Giuseppe Baglivi and John Robert Kane, trans. & eds. Binghamton, NY: CMRS, 1986.

Shaw, M.R.B., trans. *Chronicles of the Crusades*. Harmondsworth: Penguin Books, 1963.

Stevenson, Joseph, ed. *Lanercost Chronicle*. Glasgow: Maitland Club, 1839.

BIBLIOGRAPHY

Thiébaux, Marcelle, trans. and ed. *The Writings of Medieval Women.* New York: Garland Publishing, 1987.

Viorst, Milton, ed. *Great Documents of Western Civilization.* Philadelphia: Chilton Books, 1965.

SECONDARY WORKS

Adams, Carol, Paula Bertley, et al. *From Workshop to Warfare: The Lives of Medieval Women.* Cambridge: Cambridge University Press, 1983.

Arnold, Benjamin. *Princes and Territories in Medieval Germany.* Cambridge: Cambridge University Press, 1991.

Artz, Frederick B. *The Mind of the Middle Ages: An Historical Survey A.D. 200-1500.* Chicago: University of Chicago Press, 1980.

Aston, Margaret. *The Fifteenth Century: The Prospect of Europe.* New York: W.W. Norton, 1979.

Bachrach, Bernard S. and David Nicholas. *Law, Custom and Social Fabric in Medieval Europe.* Toronto: Medieval Institute, 1990.

Baldwin, John. *The Government of Philip Augustus: Foundations of French Royal Power in the Middle Ages.* Berkeley, Los Angeles & London: University of California Press, 1991.

Barker, Juliet. *The Tournament in England 1100-1400.* Rochester, NY & Woodbridge, Suffolk: Boydell and Brewer, 1986.

Bax, Ernest B. *German Society at the Close of the Middle Ages.* New York: A.M. Kelley, 1967.

Becker, Marvin B. *Civility and Society in Western Europe 1300-1600.* Bloomington & London: Indiana University Press, 1988.

Beeler, John. *Warfare in Feudal Europe 730-1200.* Ithaca, NY: Cornell University Press, 1973.

Bennett, H.S. *The Pastons and their England.* Cambridge: Cambridge University Press, 1990.

Bismaris, M.R. *The Medieval English Domestic Timber Roof.* New York: Peter Lang Publications, 1987.

Bisson, Thomas N. *The Medieval Crown of Aragon.* Oxford: Oxford University Press, 1991.

Bloch, Marc. *Feudal Society.* L.A. Manyon, trans. 2 vols. London & New York: Routledge and Kegan Paul, 1961.

Brooke, Christopher. *The Medieval Idea of Marriage*. Oxford: Oxford University Press, 1989.

Broughton, Bradford B. *Dictionary of Medieval Knighthood and Chivalry: People, Places and Events*. Westport, CT: Greenwood Press, 1988.

Brown, R. Allen. *The Architecture of Castles*. North Pomfret, VT: Trafalgar Square, 1990.

Cairns, Conrad. *The Medieval Castle*. Cambridge: Cambridge University Press, 1987.

Calmette, Joseph. *The Golden Age of Burgundy*. London: Weidenfeld and Nicolson, 1962.

Cathcart-King, D.J. *Castles in England and Wales: An Interpretative History*. Portland, OR: Areopagitica, 1988.

Chamberlin, E.R. *Life in Medieval France*. New York: G.P. Putnam, 1967.

Crowder, C.M. *English Society and Government in the Fifteenth Century*. Edinburgh and London: Oliver & Boyd, 1967.

Davies, R.R. *The British Isles 1100-1500: Comparisons, Contrasts and Connections*. Atlantic Highlands, NJ: Humanities Press, 1988.

Dronke, Peter. *Women Writers of the Middle Ages*. Cambridge: Cambridge University Press, 1984.

DuBoulay, F. *The England of Piers Plowman: William Langland and his Vision of the Fourteenth Century*. Rochester, NY & Woodbridge, Suffolk: Boydell and Brewer, 1991.

—. *Germany in the Later Middle Ages*. Atlantic Highlands, NJ: Humanities Press, 1988.

Duby, Georges. *The Knight, the Lady and the Priest*. Barbara Day, trans. Harmondsworth: Peregrine Books, 1985.

—., ed. *Revelations of the Medieval World. History of Private Life*. Vol. 2. Philippe Ariès and Georges Duby, gen. eds. Cambridge, MA: Harvard University Press, 1988.

—. *The Three Orders: Feudal Society Imagined*. Chicago: University of Chicago Press, 1980.

—. and Robert Mandrou. *A History of French Civilization*. London: Weidenfeld and Nicolson, 1964.

BIBLIOGRAPHY

Duckett, Eleanor S. *Gateway to the Middle Ages: France and Great Britain.* Ann Arbor: University of Michigan Press 1988.

Fuhrmann, Horst. *Germany in the High Middle Ages.* Cambridge: Cambridge University Press 1986.

Furnivall, Frederick James. *Early English Meals and Manners. John Russell's Boke of Nurture.* London: Oxford University Press for the Early English Text Society, 1868.

Galbraith, Vivian H. *Kings and Chronicles: Essays in English Medieval History.* London: Hambledon Press, 1982.

Gies, Francis, and Joseph Gies. *Women in the Middle Ages.* New York: Barnes & Noble, 1978.

Gies, Joseph and Frances Gies. *Life in a Medieval Castle.* New York: Harper & Row, 1974.

Hardy, Emmeline. *The Story of Corfe Castle.* New York: State Mutual, 1984.

Harper, Bill Christopher, and Ruth Harvey, eds. *Ideals and Practice of Medieval Knighthood.* Rochester, NY & Woodbridge, Suffolk: Boydell and Brewer, 1986.

Haskins, Charles Homer. *The Normans in European History.* New York: W.W. Norton, 1966.

Haverkamp, Alfred, *Medieval Germany 1056-1273.* Helga Braun and Richard Mortimer, trans. Oxford: Oxford University Press, 1988.

Herlihy, David. *Medieval Households.* Cambridge: Harvard University Press, 1985.

Hewitt, Herbert James. *The Organisation of War under Edward III, 1338-1362.* Manchester: Manchester University Press & New York: Barnes & Noble, 1966.

Hibbert, Christopher. *Agincourt.* London: B.T. Batsford, 1964.

Hindley, Geoffrey. *England in the Age of Caxton.* London & New York: St. Martin's Press, 1979.

Holmes, George, ed. *The Oxford Illustrated History of Medieval Europe.* Oxford: Oxford University Press, 1990.

Huffines, Marion L. *Stricker and Wernher: A View of Chivalry and Peasantry in Germany of the Late Middle Ages.* New York: Gordon Press, 1976.

Hyde, J.K. *Padua in the Age of Dante*. Manchester: Manchester University Press, 1966.

Jacob, Ernest. *Henry v and the Invasion of France*. London: Hodder & Stoughton for the English Universities Press, 1947.

Jameson, E. "Alliance of England and Sicily in the Second Half of the Twelfth Century." *Journal of the Warburg and Courtauld Institutes* 6 (1943): 20-23.

Jarman, Rosemary Hawley. *Crispin's Day: The Glory of Agincourt*. Boston: Little Brown, 1979.

Johnson, James. *The Just War Tradition and the Restraint of War: A Moral and Historical Inquiry*. Princeton: Princeton University Press, 1981.

Johnson, Paul. *Castles of England, Scotland and Wales*. New York: Harper Collins, 1989.

Jones, P.J. *The Malestata of Rimini and the Papal State*. Cambridge: Cambridge University Press, 1974.

Kaeuper, Richard W. *War, Justice and Public Order: England and France in the Late Middle Ages*. Oxford: Oxford University Press, 1988.

Keen, Maurice. *English Society in the Later Middle Ages 1348-1500*. New York: Viking Penguin, 1991.

Kirshner, Julius and Suzanne F. Wemple, eds. *Women of the Medieval World*. Oxford: Basil Blackwell, 1985.

Klapisch-Zuber, Christiane, ed. *Silences of the Middle Ages. A History of Women*. Vol. 2. Georges Duby and Michelle Perrot, gen. eds. Cambridge, MA: Harvard University Press, 1992.

Labarge, Margaret W.A. *A Baronial Household in the Thirteenth Century*. London: Eyre & Spottiswoode, 1965.

Lander, J.R. *The Limitations of Monarchy in the Later Middle Ages*. Toronto: University of Toronto Press, 1989.

Larner, John. *Italy in the Age of Dante and Petrarch, 1216-1380*. Longman History of Italy. Vol. 2. London & New York: Longman, 1980.

—. *The Lords of Romagna: Romagnol Society and the Origins of the Signorie*. London & New York: Longman, 1965.

Lewis, Archibald R. *Essays in Later Medieval French History*. London: Hambledon Press, 1985.

BIBLIOGRAPHY

Lucas, Angela M. *Women in the Middle Ages: Religion, Marriage and Letters.* Brighton: Harvester Press, 1984.

Martines, Lauro. *Power and Imagination: City-States in Renaissance Italy.* New York: Vintage Books, 1980.

Mason, Roger, ed. *Scotland and England 1286-1815.* Atlantic Highlands, NJ: Humanities Press, 1987.

Matthew, Donald. *The Norman Kingdom of Sicily.* Cambridge: Cambridge University Press, 1992.

Miller, William Ian. *Bloodtaking and Peacemaking: Feud, Law and Society in Saga Iceland.* Chicago: University of Chicago Press, 1990.

Mitchell, Otis. *Two German Crowns: Monarchy and Empire in Medieval Germany.* Bristol, IN: Wyndham Hall, 1985.

Neillands, Robin Hunter. *The Hundred Years' War.* New York: Routledge, 1990.

Nelson, Janet. *Politics and Ritual in Medieval Europe.* London: Hambledon Press, 1986.

Painter, Sidney. *French Chivalry.* Ithaca: Cornell University Press, 1957.

Palmer, J.J.N. *England, France and Christendom 1377-1399.* Chapel Hill: University of North Carolina Press, 1972.

Perroy, Edouard. *The Hundred Years' War.* Bloomington & London: Indiana University Press, 1959.

Platt, Colin. *Medieval England: A Social History and Archaeology from the Conquest to A.D. 1600.* New York: Routledge, 1989.

Power, Eileen. *Medieval Women.* M.M. Postan, ed. Cambridge: Cambridge University Press, 1975.

Reuter, Timothy. *Germany in the Early Middle Ages.* London & New York: Longman, 1991.

Reynolds, Susan. *Fiefs and Vassals.* Oxford: Oxford University Press, 1994.

Russell, Frederick H. *The Just War in the Middle Ages.* Cambridge & New York: Cambridge University Press, 1977.

Sanders, Ivor J. *Feudal Military Service in England: A Study of the Constitutional and Military Powers in Medieval England.* Oxford: Oxford University Press, 1956.

Seward, Desmond. *The Hundred Years War: The English in France 1337-1453*. London: Constable, 1978.

Taylor A.J. *Studies in Castles and Castle Building*. London: Hambledon Press, 1986.

Tuchman, Barbara. *A Distant Mirror: The Calamitous Fourteenth Century*. New York: Alfred A. Knopf, 1978.

Tuck, Anthony. *Richard II and the English Nobility*. London: Edward Arnold, 1973.

Waley, Daniel. *The Italian City-Republics*. London & New York: Longman, 1988.

Walker, Simon. *The Lancastrian Affinity 1361-1399*. Oxford: Oxford University Press, 1990.

Ward, Jennifer C. *English Noblewomen in the Later Middle Ages*. London & New York: Longman 1992.

Woods, William. *England in the Age of Chaucer*. New York: Stein and Day, 1976.

INDEX

INDEX

INDEX

This Book Was Completed on March 1, 1996
At Italica Press, New York, NY. It Was Set
In Adobe Charlemagne and Monotype
Dante and Printed on 50 lb Gladfelter
Natural, Acid-Free Paper with a
Smyth-Sewn Binding
By McNaughton &
Gunn, Saline,
MI, USA

★   ★

★